THE SPREZZATURA PRINCIPLES

ACHIEVING MAGICAL GOALS WITH EFFORTLESS MASTERY

SEEMINGLY DIFFICULT TASKS, MADE
EASIER WITH TECHNIQUES THAT HAVE
WORKED FOR MILLIONS

MANI M NAGASUBRAMANIAN

ISBN

Hardcase 979-8-89961-625-9
Paperback 979-8-89610-667-8

Sprezzatura [sprettsa'tuːra] is an Italian-origin word that has entered the English language; **'making difficult tasks seem effortless'** is a simpler meaning in a gist.

It is a certain nonchalance so as to conceal all effort and make whatever one does or says appear to be without effort and almost without any thought about it.

It is the ability to display 'an easy facility in accomplishing difficult actions which hides the conscious effort that went into them'.

Sprezzatura: apparent reticence and studied nonchalance

PRINCIPLES are understood truths or propositions so clear that they cannot be proved nor contradicted

A fundamental truth or proposition that serves as the foundation for a system of belief or behavior or for a chain of reasoning.

A principle is a kind of rule, belief, or idea that guides you.

Title: The **SPREZZATURA** Principles

Mani M. Nagasubramanian

The hook: Seemingly DIFFICULT, made easier with techniques that have worked for millions.

The word: "difficult" is implied to include all the tasks, arts, hobbies, work inter alia. So, all that is considered difficult is made easier.

Book Precis: (unedited)

+ Be your original self and celebrate life in abundant joy and success.

Lead your life in your own way, style, and fashion.

+ Discover your innate strengths and skills.

Realize your true identity, image, and self.

+ Build on your values and virtues by yourself.

+ Celebrate fun, fashion, fine art, gourmet foods, and epicurean luxury.

Whatever you desire, you deserve as your birthright.

+ Disciplined pursuit of the essential few

Mind is burdened with borrowed thoughts of other people's views, ideas, and even shortcomings at the cost of our own ability to soar.

Our own way of thinking and dormant intelligence should be awakened from within. There's an enormous potential or wealth of unused substance available in each of us.

Such intelligence is a blessing, and life is simpler and more natural when progressing through the light of one's own intelligence. There is no possibility of chaos and licentiousness.

There is no suppression, only a natural revelation of inner beauty and harmony.

When we live our lives with borrowed thoughts or to conform to others' diktats, philosophies, and trends, our life itself is borrowed, make-believe. Get out of that habit, something most of us have acquired under some frivolous presumption for supremacy or even endorsement by an extraneous, virtual, and mysterious force! Be your natural self with your own thoughts, learning, and your spontaneous being. You will see an amazingly new life, a brand-new world of great potential and possibilities in your personal and professional life.

When we connect with our true selves and nature, beautiful evolutions erupt and manifest. Here again, don't get deluded by others' opinions, extraneous trends, fads, airy and fairy theories to realize what happiness is for you. Your happiness, joy, and success are independent of others' support, endorsement, or approval. From our childhood, this has been inculcated as a holy habit. Let's get out of that habit and any that have been acquired unknowingly, oblivious to the true reality of ourselves.

CONTENTS

WHAT I WANT FOR MY READERS IS...

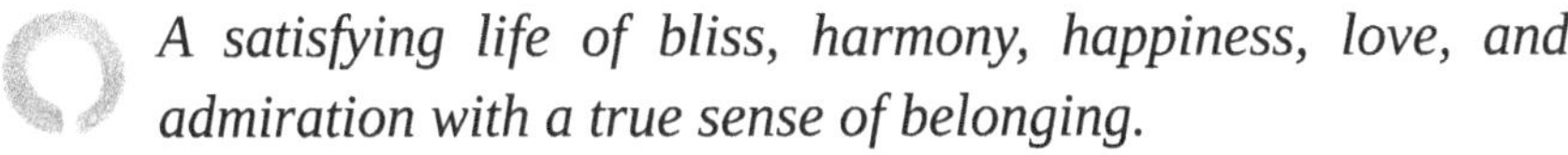 *A satisfying life of bliss, harmony, happiness, love, and admiration with a true sense of belonging.*

All these may appear superficial, hard to get, or lofty and over-ambitious.

In fact, these aspects are simply possible because they are meant to be simple. You deserve them.

We are making it complex, giving unnecessary dimensions, fitting them into complex theories, and categorizing them as difficult with labels of popular terms or jargon.

There is no need to waste time evaluating or figuring out what life is, whether it is good or bad, right or wrong, and so on. The very evaluation is wrong because there's no need to wonder about any of our life's experiences. It's merely a habit; a bad habit. Life is as it is; it has been, but varied and complex meanings or dimensions are given by people.

Instead, accept and embrace them as they happen with total confidence that they are as they are meant to be, with the understanding that we do need a variety/mix of such variations and features to make our lives better and have a beautiful perspective, which, in fact, would resolve all the mystery and magically bring joy into our lives. Find unity in variety. Choose to celebrate the present when you don't waste your time evaluating, judging, and classifying life's happenings.

Life's value, importance, and worth are not measured by its duration. People waste and waste their lives and time thinking about the future all the time. This is absurd. When we do this, we escape from now, wasting the present. What is important is how we spend, celebrate, and be in the present, doing whatever is given. Life is not a possession to be owned one way or the other. None of us needs to have control, command, or ownership of it. Why do you need to 'own' it anyway, like the way you choose to want to own myriad things? Time, the present is more important and valuable than all the other material things put together. After all, we get one life.

Life certainly is not something else to be owned.

* * *

THE BIG PROMISE

Celebrate your life in abundance of joy and success with just the one insight or principle that SPREZZATURA would empower you with: Stay in the present, and live your life fully by 'thinking' appropriately, i.e., by regulating your thoughts with conscious/mindful breathing.

Get clarity on your definitive purpose.

Discover your innate skill and strength.

There's no need to postpone happiness.

A very, very important aspect of The Sprezzatura Principles is its role as a simple guide to self-knowledge. Identify your core values, capability, and naturalness. This quality is something you have always felt out of reach, imagined you don't deserve, or couldn't express. Much that is simple is made complex over a period of time for reasons beyond our need to know or worry about.

Everything you need to become your best version is well within yourself for the taking.

Sprezzatura is an immensely sophisticated accumulation of the experiences of select philosophy, principles, and people presented in an interesting, fashionable, and easy form with practical guidance for tangible benefits. Voices of others engage and stretch your notion of yourself in the world.

At first, much of a good, happy, and successful life seems difficult and belongs to others, but be assured to discover that you have all the ideas and attitudes that make your own ways and means to enrich yourself.

Sprezzatura is a discovery of YOU – a restoration of your immense portent potential at your pace.

What we think of ourselves and of the world makes us who we are and what we can be. There is nothing good or bad.

We can always try to think differently.

It is the return of an ancient habit:

The greatest virtue is to be yourself in a world that constantly tries to make you someone or even something else.

One of the fundamental precepts of SPREZZATURA is that we need to reconnect with ourselves and see ourselves in totality as the ground truth.

A

HERE AND NOW

We cannot devote ourselves to the here and now when we are caught up in producing results. This makes us focus and live in the future! It is smarter to choose to be in the present, here and now. Doing whatever needs to be done or you have chosen to do without wasting time or energy on the results, and their benefits in the future keeps you away from anxieties. This way of life leads to better and more appropriate results. There is no other or better way. When thinking and living in the here and now, be assured that there's no better way than what you are already up to. Being selfish, greedy, and insecure focuses on the benefits of the future results, wasting the beautiful now.

B

PRIORITY AND ACTIVITY

Time management is prioritizing activities and their management in optimal time. Choose the right activities first. This may sound simple, but it is not because our personal favorites and even ego needs take precedence.

Be wary of that habit and act smarter to prioritize those natural and complementary to one's values, purpose, and core competencies. After prioritizing comes the all-important allocation of time. This needs caution. Just because one of the priority events, items, or tasks is important does not mean all the time is given to it. Oftentimes, this happens to everyone. Think about effectiveness and efficiency, too.

Make it a point to identify the key, important, and urgent need, which cannot be more than **one**. Priority is singular and cannot be given simultaneously in the plural!

On completion, move on to the next, just one at a time.

C

WORK FOR INFLUENCE – NOT RECOGNITION.

Contribute and create, really making a 'difference' to others. This could be to individuals thoughtfully and effectively or for a cause that affects several. Help others in meaningful ways. Here, the word 'meaningful' means a lot. Focus on understanding the root cause of the situation and the person(s) before considering or offering to help. This way, you are better prepared to use your resources and time effectively.

You will be amazed at the wonders of what it does to you over a period of time. This may sound cosmic or supernatural, yet redundant words make the innate significance and qualities beyond explanation.

D

DON'T DEMONSTRATE TO BE RIGHT. INSTEAD, REROUTE

Have you noticed how Google Maps never yells, condemns, or castigates you if you take the wrong turn? It never raises its voice and says, "You were supposed to go LEFT at the last crossing, you idiot! Now you're going to have to go the LONG way around, and it's going to take you SO much more time, and you're going to be late for your meeting! Learn to pay attention and listen to my instructions, OK???" If it did that, chances are, a lot of us might stop using it. But Google simply reroutes and shows you the next best way to get there. Its primary interest is in getting you to reach your goal, not in making you feel bad for having made a mistake. There's always a possibility of those who have made a mistake, especially those who are close to us and familiar with us. But the wisest choice is to help in fixing the problem, not to blame. Have you had rerouting moments recently? With others and also with your own self?

In other words, rerouting means anything other than a big or small 'No'. Keep in mind that the word 'no' negates and even questions several other things and aspects in the other person's life! Though your intention was to tell someone that you are not the right person for something they sought from you – came to you for. Rightfully, you do not have the expertise and it may be beyond your circle of competence. The problem is the way the word 'NO' is perceived or transliterated in the worst possible ways on each individual's whim, fancy or accord. Instead, REROUTE.

Your intent and idea are to succeed ultimately and mutually, are they not? Success does not imply failure to another.

To send by a new or different route and a brand-new approach, a new possibility, reroute is defined as sending something in a new or different direction. An example of reroute is giving a piece of mail that came to your house by mistake back to the postal service to be returned. To change the route taken by something.

Look at the following synonyms of your best defense weapon or word: reroute.

None of them means negative, bad, wrong or *mean*.

When you don't have a solution, can't do a thing, or when you can't accept to do it–neither say no nor return it. Send the request or person along a different path than usual, instead. Simple. Just deflect it.

E

INNER VOICE

Chatters, Clamors, Commotions and Cacophonies keep your focus and concentration away from your innate interests and values.

Imagine your feelings of inner chatter and clutter as common and similar to what others experience regularly. There is nothing unusual or wrong with them.

We are much better at advising other people than ourselves. Try thinking of yourself as someone else and coach, train, and lecture that person–again, the 'yourself' in the way you have enjoyed advising others.

How can we stop recalling the past, especially all the negative events and people? Self-doubt is a habit, a terrible bad habit.

This tends to happen often due to silly triggers or reasons.

To get out of this bad habit, one of the best ways is to learn a new skill or hobby that makes us inventive and helps us discover a new fizz in our lives, a revelation of our own potential.

Transform any unexpected event, unplanned outcome or circumstance into an opportunity for new actions and outcomes and better results.

Even a pandemic lockout—or any such unexpected situation—warrants and demands that we change our ways of doing things. This is not to be labeled as 'bad', as the very label makes it so.

This just means one needs to be ready to change one's habitual routines, most of which are mindless and on autopilot!

Don't call a situation names just because it demands you to change from your list of comfortable routines.

Stop complaining about the newly evolved chance and opportunity to think, plan, and do anything differently in a better or smarter way.

Unwillingness to accept the new is common for humans as they are more comfortable with the all-too-known past, as familiarity gives a sense of comfort even though it is certainly not a sign of progress.

F

RITUALS

Rituals can provide us with a sense of order. They can, at most, help direct our attention and energy away from the problem towards possible solutions.

It shapes our subconscious mind. It also helps practice whatever you've chosen to perfection.

Practicing anything chosen as essential is important, and when carried out in a pattern or modus operandi, you are, in fact, making it a ritual. Period.

Rituals encourage you to focus on one important thing at a time. Practice that one consistently, long enough to perfect it and see glory: a beautiful outcome or revelation.

Don't we all remember that our parents told us to take an oil bath on Saturdays, cut nails on Sundays and never after sunset, and pray at home or in a temple, church, or mosque on a specific day? Rituals have some inexplicable meaning and benefit humanity, and even the economy is positively affected by them.

When you follow the rituals, you tend to stay in the here and now. Oh! What a great feeling!

The by-products and benefits are to complete what is started.

It is very easy to come up with great ideas, as it may sound in the beginning; most of them sound promising to kick-start. But to complete the task, any single activity needs a ritualistic approach of discipline and consistency, combined with passion and love.

1

YOU HAVE TO HAVE 'ONE' GOAL: A DEFINITIVE PURPOSE

It is important to have a definitive purpose that is beyond, greater, and mightier than your selfish interests.

Most of the time, we are conditioned to search greedily for various and myriad sets of goods to feel good. This includes titles, places to visit and recognition from people who really do not matter. You need not waste time going after such horrendous and extraneous stuff that is distant and difficult; a needless activity because even if you succeed in that exercise, you will not be assured of peace, harmony, success and xyz. Because 'those' things and that list of wishful items may not complement your original purpose. In other words, those things, stuff and people do not deserve you. It cannot be emphasized further that whatever we think we must have and do with specific things and certain people, we end up wasting our total energy. It is a colossal waste, an endless game of pity and humility. Please be wary of those superficialities that do not deserve your time, effort and uniqueness. When such stuff is searched for with longing and desperate eagerness, you end up in misery, worry and troubles of all kinds. The paradox is that when you achieve those alien/extraneous factors fully or partially, you would yet end up with disappointment very soon. Then your search continues on and on for something else new and far away, as in the past.

Instead, learn to connect with time, spirits, your innate, definitive purpose. With that strength, whatever you do, wherever you are, with whomever you are, life will be bliss; total ecstasy.

You are meant to do that one thing, which when it is in sync with your subconscious intent, the outcome will be natural. Discover your intent, that special one you are meant to do, which is bound to succeed.

Formulate a routine to transform life for the original and definitive purpose as intended.

Believe in it and be consistent with your efforts. Routines then play a big role.

Things in the surroundings may change, but be after your own goal, desire, and purpose.

An important trick or aspect that's hidden in any of such efforts is that when it is approached and worked on consistently, the practical or ground reality changes or evolves as the outcome would reveal on its own accord.

This is not to simplify the process and to assure or assume you of success when 'IT' is pursued in a consistent manner.

I cannot and don't want to emphasize the importance of the belief in oneself in true allegiance and congruence to the original idea that has been persistent in you; persisted in your consciousness, whatever that may be.

It would evolve to take shape, form, and pattern, style, and that's part of how anything of significance has ever been born.

Rest assured.

Scientists all over the world stumble upon discovery or invent something during their journey and process of pursuing something of high importance within or related to their discovery or invention! But if they had not set out to pursue 'that' original purpose and intent, they would not have succeeded in discovering or identifying 'this', which, in fact, is new and equally as important.

What is your primary, or rather **the only goal** or purpose?

Have one, figure out one, and let it be big, audacious, and strong.

A purpose that complements your core desires, competencies, and values. All our successes have everything to do with focusing on our core desires.

It is unfortunate that the word 'desire' is ambiguously referred to and understood in a negative sense in its practical usage.

Conversely, desire is learning how to unleash and use your conquering force, that crucial ingredient is vital to your success in anything: making money, improving relationships, boosting self-esteem, gaining confidence and more. It all comes from the amazing and conquering force within each of us. Once you destroy all invisible obstacles such as fear, self-doubt, lack of confidence or esteem, wrong paradigms, opinions or fear of failure, your life will flow automatically or naturally, fulfilling your desire, goal and purpose.

You can become a peak performer in any area of life that matters to you. A **definitive purpose** is the outcome of a strong desire. Now, let's get practical as in the style of a workshop:

List three reasons why you should achieve your goal.

List three things that you will lose if you don't reach your goal.

List three beliefs that have held you back from reaching your goal.

What has stopped you? What beliefs would help you to achieve your goal? Could you replace the negative beliefs with the positive?

To make it easier for yourself to make these new empowering beliefs a part of your reality, create a list of role models—people who have already reached what you want to achieve or who are expressions of the belief you need to reach your goal. If possible, make a list of things in your direct experience or surroundings that confirm your empowering belief. If obstacles appear, it might indicate that your goal is not in alignment with your life mission; as simple as that. Nothing to worry about. What you categorize as obstacles stem from your past limiting beliefs.

Pessimism, procrastination, and postponement are impediments to progress and prosperity. A well-defined purpose would drive away all those P factors.

I have set myself or identified my purpose as my desire to help and make a big difference in others' lives. Let's say for which I would need to enhance my income and wealth by over ten times. Here's the hidden secret and trick. One doesn't need that much wealth stored in a bank or home to set a goal and define one's definitive purpose. The beginning is from the purpose. It's as simple as that to make things happen.

(The scientific reasons, quantum physics, and cognition are not meant to be elaborated here *(in this book)* to substantiate this point)

It is important to have a 'definitive purpose' that's beyond, big and mightier than your selfish or short-sighted mind.

Here again, what is your ONE special, specific goal, purpose, and desire?

Or even a combination of all in ONE.

This 'one' ought to be something you choose to live for, be passionate about, and leave behind for posterity.

There is no need to feel small or humbled by these words or, for that matter, anyone's theory/formula because each of us is far more competent, capable, and powerful/bigger than we choose to accept to set our goals. All the accomplished people and millionaires say the same thing: "Oh... I didn't think BIG, didn't aim for multiples of what I have achieved and similar."

Why?

The reason is when the chosen goal is right and relevant to one's definitive purpose, interests, and complementary to one's skills, traits, and so on, it is bound to be achieved. Of course, persistence plays its important role and it pays.

It may take multiple attempts; let's give it a figure: 10. Yes, ten attempts.

When you intend and are ready to go for it ten times with sustained interest, you are likely to realize it much earlier. This is based on and endorsed by those who have done and gone the distance and won/achieved in their lives with their determined one definitive purpose.

Do the unexpected from your usual self; do more and differently, preparing multiple, simultaneous alternatives in your efforts to reach the objective. Believe in your hidden and often ignored expertise. It is smarter to take all the unconventional, uncommon, and indirect routes to your objective.

Apply/focus on your individualistic ONE objective and self; first, and your profession, job or company, et al., will be taken care of automatically.

Paying attention to your 'self' does not make you selfish.

The person or the obvious priority, the objective/purpose, is seldom given importance because we are habitually blind to our own blindness and ignorance.

Take care of your objective, your definitive purpose to see the results and celebrate life.

Live a life of definitive PURPOSE.

A purpose is a master plan for our life.

Knowing our purpose helps to define our goals.

It makes life more enjoyable and effortless.

The purpose is not something that others choose for us.

We must choose it for ourselves.

Your purpose is your connection to something larger, something that will allow you to make your mark in the world, to truly make a difference.

You want more zest, more fullness, greater happiness.

You want to wake up in the morning excited and enthusiastic, jumping out of bed with a thirst for life that you haven't felt since you were a child.

To begin with, you need to expand your mind.

Read inspiring stories of others who achieved greatness.

Read the scriptures.

Invest your time in helping others.

Another's pain can lead you to awareness of all that you are blessed with.

Cultivate a sense of awe and gratitude.

When you connect with your inner self, the divine power, you are driven to make a positive impact on the world.

WHAT'S YOUR SINGULAR AND UNIQUE GOAL?

IDENTIFY AND COMBINE YOUR GOAL AND INNATE SKILLS TO LIVE YOUR LIFE FULLY

<u>2</u>

THOUGHTS, THOUGHTS, AND THOUGHTS

We humans have anywhere from 12,000 to 60,000 thoughts per day. But according to some research, as many as 98 percent of them are exactly the same as we had the day before (and even months and years earlier!). Talk about creatures of habit! Even more significantly, 80 percent of our thoughts are negative.

Our **thoughts** shape our minds and our life, its future and destiny. One's way of thinking can attract health or sickness, gain or loss, affluence or poverty.

Your actions, in quantity, class, sophistication, and quality, are entirely decided by your thoughts, the quality of thoughts, to be specific.

In fact, when you consciously choose to think less and less, there will be an incredible and joyous outcome: the quality of your thoughts will go up tremendously. This leads to appropriate action and a well-lived life.

Beware of your thoughts, but don't attach yourself to any of them or with your wild imaginations on your thoughts' outcome. After all, they are your thoughts and thoughts only. Stop giving them real-life meaning and your imaginative projections. The quality and variety of thinking and activities determine our lives.

Watch out for the kind of people and type or quality of conversations we have. This is very, very important. Negative thoughts *en masse* are a virus with no vaccination or cure. Keep in mind and believe that your thoughts, positive, relevant or negative, function as a program of your mind's PC and that could transform your whole self.

Thoughts lead to beliefs, desires, and actions. Self-mastery of our thoughts is a certain and surefire way to lead a successful and happy life.

Right thinking turns us to our original nature.

We all need to change our lifestyles with the right, relevant, and our original thinking.

Become what and who you are meant to be.

All of us can do that. After all, we are the ones who think and can decide what's right for us, right?

We need to be convinced that the creator is the one living inside us.

We can change any of our situations by way of thinking, re-planning, and discovering the true self and its lessons. With hope and your own right thinking, make your goal a fulfilling life, and it will manifest in unexpected ways. Synchronicity or whatever you might want to call it.

The sun, which is hidden right behind the shade or cloud, is waiting to come out and back you up with full force.

We need to develop positive thinking in ourselves as a habit. We must forget that we faced darkness yesterday. We should only focus on the light and not darkness.

So, don't we need to take care of and nurture our thoughts?

How do we shape the quality and efficacy of our thoughts?

Isn't it necessary, and is it possible?

Work on your thoughts, yourself... For empowerment to get out of the unawareness and ignorance of reality.

We can change this. The first step is to stay away from the typical, mechanically framed, fabricated news, campaigns, and propaganda with borrowed phrases. Borrowed phrases are just fashionable statements, merely borrowed to make them sound interesting and convincing. I hate the overload of quotes from famous people, often brought about in the image, expectation and hope of strengthening one's otherwise empty and hollow words.

Words are the next very important aspect, whose power is underrated or unknown.

We, humans, are fond of using words that are **unaccountable,** netted with unaccountable, unnatural, and unnecessary vibrations of useless words, tuneless, disharmonious sounds, and frivolous thoughts produced by exploiting the available ways and means of 'media'/communication channels to the maximum. The excessive use of redundant sounds or words is an innate tendency, often driven by selfish motives or artificially acquired habits—forcefully adopted simply because they are freely available. A selfish and egotistic expression, born out of total ignorance habitually.

Instead, connect with nature and **be** and **do** what comes naturally to you. Stop looking outward to endorse yourself; it's redundant and useless. You really do not need any of those words of wisdom or fashionably famous and frivolous endorsements.

Get into the habit of meditation or whatever it is that puts you in your true spirit and natural being.

Pay more attention to habits, such as food, than words! Follow certain and the age-old wisdom of eating on time for every meal, having the right and well-balanced nutrition, and eating foods without preservatives to detox your body and mind, a natural and incredible evolution.

Let's realize the importance of being natural, spontaneous, and original as we were meant to be.

You become who you think you are through repetitive thoughts and visualizations. This whole world is made of thoughts.

It is proven that mindfulness meditation and creative visualization strengthen certain parts of the brain by generating fresh brain cells, neurons, and synapses, or connections between neurons. Scientific evidence leads to the same point. Most stubborn mental disorders like Obsessive Compulsive Disorder and Depression can be cured with the help of meditation and creative visualization. By mindfully and objectively witnessing the thoughts without reacting, you could get over any kind of thoughts and emotions, both positive and negative. Yes, become equanimous to objectively celebrate life as a brand-new 'you'.

<u>3</u>
DON'T OUTSOURCE YOUR THINKING

Most of us have no problem thinking about what we want to achieve in life, at least when we're young. We're full of big dreams, big ideas, and boundless energy. The problem is that we let others tell us what's possible and what isn't, not only when it comes to our dreams but also when it comes to how we go about realizing them. And when we let other people tell us what's possible or what the best way to do something is, we outsource our thinking to someone else.

'The Sprezzatura Principles' thinking is one of the best ways to reverse-engineer complicated problems and unleash creative possibilities. The idea is to break down complicated problems into basic elements and then reassemble them from the ground up. It's one of the best ways to learn to think for yourself, unlock your creative potential, and move from linear to non-linear results.

It doesn't matter if this approach was used by the philosopher Aristotle, or it is now used by Elon Musk and Charlie Munger. It allows us to cut through the fog of shoddy reasoning and inadequate analogies to see opportunities that others miss.

If we never learn to take something apart, test the assumptions, and reconstruct it, we end up trapped in what other people tell us, trapped in the way things have always been done. When the environment changes, we just continue as if things were the same.

Sprezzatura principles' reasoning cuts through dogmas and removes the blinders. We can see the world as it is and see what is possible.

When it comes down to it, everything that is not a law of nature is just a shared belief. Money is a shared belief. So is a border. The list goes on.

Some of us are naturally skeptical of what we're told. Maybe it doesn't match up to our experiences. Maybe it's something that used to be true but isn't anymore. And maybe we just think very differently about something. So be it and be happy.

<u>4</u>

BALANCE
DON'T EVER COPY, COMPETE, COMPARE, CRITICIZE, COMPLAIN OR COMPROMISE

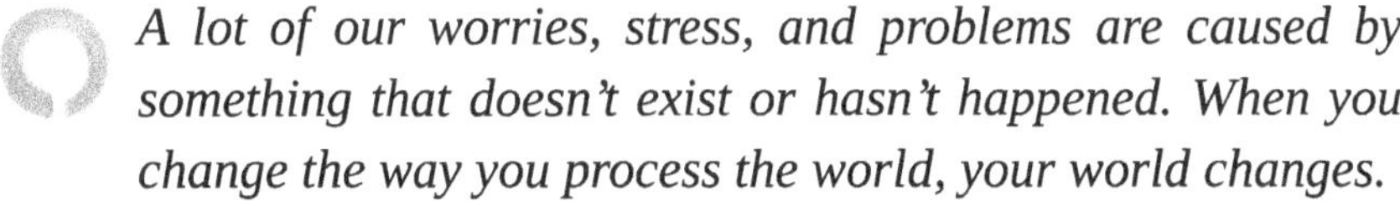 *A lot of our worries, stress, and problems are caused by something that doesn't exist or hasn't happened. When you change the way you process the world, your world changes.*

Include in your life an elaborate variety of activities that are easy, fun, and even provocative; it's all up to you.

But if you don't, no amount of any of the following would help: Visits to holy places, chanting mantras, exercises, nature, and umpteen such activities; including the new age, new world, emerging pseudo-fashionable trends.

You become what you constantly think about all day long. The incredible and inevitable insight is that your negative, stressful thoughts and apprehensions have immense potential to manifest simply, easily, and beautifully all that you have been thinking all day long.

Align your thoughts with the success you are capable of attracting through the strength of your convictions so that the negative thoughts and results will not affect or take you away for a ride from your innate balanced life. Don't focus on speed, acceleration, various metrics of success, and so on to remain balanced. Your own chosen life, well-lived, is what you truly deserve as per your desires. Why are you finding fault in that?

What you most need to learn is how to create a balance between what it is that you desire and the thoughts and energy you are choosing to attract to realize those in total balance with confidence.

Refrain from seeking, looking outward for solutions, and getting dependent on remedies and medications for symptoms of presumed problems or situations that are obviously not real. Getting into balance isn't necessarily about changing your behavior. You can pursue stress-reducing activities such as meditation, exercises, walks along the beaches, staying in nature, or whatever else works and suits you. **Stop comparing, complaining, copying, criticizing, convincing, and competing.**

Mind by itself is so very complex that so many millions of minds have chosen as a profession and business to mind others' minds. We are all born with one beautiful, unconditional, and simply wonderful mind. Period. But over a period of time, scores of rascal/ rogue minds have conspired to pollute our simple and wonderful minds. In the unsolicited bargain, we have lost our minds. We are corrupted, totally polluted, left lost and confused with assumptions and presumptions of myriad minds that act in tandem hopelessly or wastefully.

Conversely, successful people—the millionaire-mindset kind— constantly acquire specialized knowledge and skills related to their definitive purpose and their breakthrough goals. That's why you should not follow any trend or what's fashionably popular among your peers or as popularized by the media. You are gifted with a specific skill, knowledge, or capability. Constantly make efforts and enjoy perfecting your own gift. You will be amazed.

<u>5</u>

LIVE IN A WORLD OF TOTAL IGNORANCE OF WHAT'S IMPOSSIBLE

Every Breath you take is the Right Time for Great Possibilities

If you don't know something is impossible, it is easier to do!

And when nobody has done it before, they haven't made up rules to stop you from doing that. Yet they would forewarn you with unwarranted, redundant, and useless advice hinting at disastrous consequences. In any matter, if a couple of people had done something earlier, correctly or not, they would have made sufficient noise and sought attention to propagate their experience and reflections based on their specific and limited knowledge, limited to anyone's imagination or capabilities. That cannot define the rule to limit you from doing your stuff, a dream of impossibility. Because that's how anything new has ever been attempted and accomplished: live in the world of possibilities with total ignorance about what is impossible.

A normal person breathes 21,600 times in a day. Did you know that it encourages you to make conscious choices in the present? Besides, of course, reminding you to stay in the present. Hope and power lie in the present moment's conscious choices. Every breath you take is an opportunity to create the presence of wellness for the great potential of a beautiful life. Every breath you take is a gift to celebrate the here and now and fill it with the right choices, making the right connections. The quality of our lives is decided by and dependent on the quality of relationships and experiences.

6
UPDATE YOUR BELIEFS

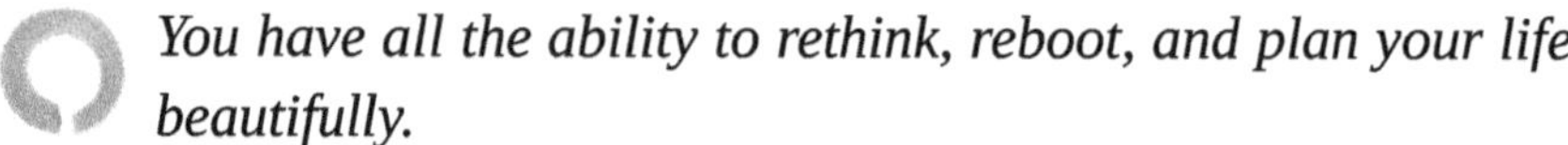 *You have all the ability to rethink, reboot, and plan your life beautifully.*

To learn anything new and unique or special, it is important to unlearn first and make way and space.

Like the way you need to declutter your wardrobe, home, workstation and such periodically, it is equally or more important to get rid of your habitual activities, routines and even the people, yes! To update your life, you have to simplify or get rid of the mess, disorder, complications, clutter and confusion. It is irritatingly interesting and incredible that most of the wasteful stuff we do is on autopilot without our conscious knowledge, involvement or interest.

Throw away non-productive items and also habitual activities, and even people, more frequently from now on.

Don't close your mind to what you don't know.

We have a tendency to close our minds to what we don't know or don't like. This leads us to brand what we don't know much about as anything we don't like and bad, too. This is a dangerous mindset to remain antiquated, rigid, and unhappy, a stereotypical behavior commonly followed by most, unaware of its malignancy and compound cause of portent problems.

It is easier to update your beliefs and mind when you abandon some of the most routines in the name of the favorite parts of your activity and identity. Conversely, stay open and be willing to flow comfortably with new, uncertain and seemingly risky or dangerous!

In fact, consciously make efforts to experience new things in every walk of life to give yourself an opportunity to grow more, a revelation to express your inner and hidden talents, traits and interests. One never knows the portent potential unless it is given an opportunity to bloom. What other way is possible to set your mind on beliefs? The simple and easy way is to fill your mind with new experiences and ideas. Of course, you are the master, boss and sole authority to choose what complements your being, whereabouts, profession and the current life stage.

Pick and choose what draws your interest and intention after the cursory exposure to all things new. If you concentrate with genuine interest, even a phone book or a company's business brochure can be interesting. If you are bored, maybe you are not concentrating sufficiently.

New things, when indulged with your own genuine interest, give you joy and an indirect benefit. More essential or important is that you would end up staying in the present and savoring every moment as it goes by. In other words, worries, apprehensions, doubts, and fears are kept away.

Oh! What a beautiful life, then.

And if you find yourself interacting with people who leave you feeling not so good about yourself, you should avoid them— or minimize your time with them—in the future,

Truth, like gold, is to be obtained not by its growth but by washing away from it all that is **not** gold or truth.

When our greed is awakened, we are cheated or rather deceived, especially when we listen and believe it blindly. Be wary of that self-deception.

7
THE BIG PROBLEM

 *You know much more than what you think or can tell.*

The problem is in finding what you know.

A rediscovery tool and means to destroy our presumed mask or imagery and save us from our habitually spoiled, typical disregard undermining our own innate, resilient, and resourceful capability is mandatory. Recover your sensitivity to look at your old self in new ways. We have been woefully made to assume that novelty and glamour are the only solutions and the answers or solutions are somewhere far, far away in the distant lands with special people enjoying certain privileges. All those are rubbish, and the problem is that we have been led to believe a life and world of deception, a *'maaya'* (illusory) we are accustomed to believe.

Our physical health affects our intellectual and emotional vitality, and our attitudes can affect our physical well-being. Sprezzatura addresses mind, body, and soul.

Equally important is the work you do to keep your mind young. Laughter has a huge impact on aging. So does intellectual curiosity. Meditation provides significant benefits to the physical body.

Step out of your habitual routines, rethink your paths, and revisit the passions you left behind or never acknowledged and pursued at all.

<u>8</u>
STOP RUNNING

We need to stop running.

Have you noticed that our minds constantly go after something else, someone, or another place and time when we are with whoever, doing whatever?

This running of the mind is due to our search for something or the other that is better, without ever knowing what it is that we are running after.

Develop a deep longing in the heart to get closer and get connected with your inner and original *(divine)* self.

This is possible through sitting in silence and growing in the spirit of humility.

Spend some time in silence every day and ask yourself the questions again and again:

What am I?

Where have I come?

Where is my true belonging?

What is the purpose of my visit to this world?

One day, the answer will come to you out of the depths within, and you will be revealed the secret of life.

You will know you're in your unique and special zone of genius, creating that which is at once shockingly new and completely familiar (popular) when people admire but have no idea how you do what you do,

Let alone how they can reverse-engineer it.

When an object is desired, the ego feels that you are lacking something to be found outside in the material world of objects.

The mind appears dissatisfied. This is a common phenomenon for everybody and needs to be ignored or eliminated.

When an object of desire is attained, then for the moment, the restless ego has subsided, you feel a sense of accomplishment, and consciousness seems unified.

Thus, the truth of self within the heart shines out as peace and happiness.

But though achievement of desire brings a state of happiness, such happiness or satisfaction can never last; for the ego rises up again, inherently dissatisfied and seeks some further alien things.

Human minds want changes forever, constantly seeking changes and variety in all aspects of life. It is totally peculiar and vulgar but entirely avoidable or rather should be avoided.

Avoiding temptation altogether is easier than overcoming it in various ways and means.

Like the way we focus on what we don't have (instead of appreciating what we have), we focus on what we may lose, rather than what we may gain.

Think of and visualize yourself earning the kind of money needed, the kind of lifestyle you would enjoy and realize what you deserve and never what you don't want.

The more work you put into something, the more ownership you begin to feel for it. Options distract us from the main objective. Stay focused instead.

<u>9</u>
ACCEPT YOURSELF

 *Let's accept ourselves, which may sound easy but we are not used to... There's only one reality: our true nature with infinite power.*

You may choose to meditate on the various images of deities, their names, mantras, qualities, and actions if you are comfortable with that, and it comes naturally and easily. The whole purpose is to ensure we are enabled to recognize and connect with ourselves; a beautiful revelation to express our own formidable potential, *some call it God or Godliness!?*

To do anything in life, we need to believe in ourselves and to start any journey we require grit, passion, and persistence. Yet when we look at our own 'shortcomings', we are unable to face the vicissitudes of life. When we focus on our inabilities, weaknesses, and faults, we wish to run away from them. We need to accept that each and every one of us possesses different and unique talents and capabilities.

Acceptance of oneself and to convert the awkwardness into uniqueness is vital. Our 'disability' or difficulty in a given aspect or dimension need not be and certainly not a great limitation. If we put our mind to it, we can convert that to a positive attribute, making us differently-abled and uniquely positioned. Project yourself as a Unique Selling Personality; after all, each of us is one unique, beautiful, and special person. We can make a difference because we are different. Let us learn to accept ourselves for who we are and to express ourselves in our own unique manner and style with a purpose, something to explore and choose from within. You will be amazed.

Have the confidence of self-acceptance and connect with yourself. Remain motivated and enthusiastic, come what may, and know that despite what we may consider a difficulty, we possess an innate power to make ourselves different and exceptionally great.

Most people don't like who they are and what they are doing right now. Hence, they try to escape from the current situation, getting into a victim mindset, blaming others for all the troubles, failures, and their ineptness. Please don't ever get into that abysmal belief and mindset, ever.

Instead, accept the moment and find ways to make it better and more beautiful.

How you perceive your life is how you will process it.

In the science of Martial Arts and as applicable in life, there is no such thing as 'difficult'.

Either something is possible or not possible.

When you have set yourself a goal, however big or small, in any sphere and phase, make efforts, practicing persistently and patiently, and you will be successful.

The difficulty has to ease and disappear with your consistent efforts and practice, with total belief and confidence in yourself.

Focus on the desired result, outcome, and benefits, constantly focusing on those rather than on the difficulties and the time you need to put in learning and practicing a thing, anything. If we had not learned the alphabets when we were young, we wouldn't be able to read, speak, or write. Without learning or doing what is essential with consistent effort, it is vague, crazy, and stupid to complain.

There's no such thing as hard. If you are doing something with difficulty, that means you are learning.

If your goal or a thing is complementary to your true self and nature, there is no such thing as impossible or irrelevant. Conversely, you will enjoy that process, motion, and belonging. Anything that is done with enthusiasm and joy over long enough a period would certainly result in mastery of what is chosen; secondly accruing phenomenal benefits to others as well.

Now here comes the most important SPREZZATURA principle to give you practical guidance:

If it is impossible despite your efforts and practice, accept it and move on happily.

There is no need to pursue further with constant complaints, excuses, and justifications which are out of sheer habit.

After all, if 'that' which you had attempted is not in alignment with your true self, you are going to take longer to succeed or it is not meant for you. This doesn't mean anything is wrong with you, your intellectual capacities, or integrity.

It's just that you had not visualized or evaluated or understood its misfit or irrelevance to you. Period. That's all.

Change your routine and behavior and be ready for what you deserve, which is awaiting you to discover.

When you find and accept your true 'self' as you are, you will find peace, harmony, and joy within.

Positivity and success are the natural outcome of this self-discovery.

<u>10</u>

BE THOUGHTLESS!

As often as possible or at least don't hold on to them

Original ideas and creativity happen when we are thoughtless, also known as 'flow'.

Flow happens when you just let it happen without overthinking.

In fact, your best comes when you STOP thinking.

The real masters of any kind of art practice incessantly time and again; a boring task for a common person.

But the real creators and masters enjoy the process, the ways and means, and most importantly, they refrain from seeking the results, outcomes, or benefits.

The latter is a critically important trait to focus on and go with the flow.

If you are keen on the benefits of the end result, during the process of trying, practicing, and doing for a seemingly indefinite period of time, you are bound to fail.

This takes you to the important aspect of creativity.

After rigorous practice, when you reach a point of thoughtless tiredness—almost to the point of pain—your real creativity evolves. This is true in every aspect of creative life.

Even in Martial Arts, one is enticed to practice certain rigorous physical tasks repeatedly to a point of gruesome pain. At that point, your mind is totally thoughtless but to do the given task, job or goal.

A beautiful happenstance occurs then.

You will be blissfully thoughtless with no fear, anxiety, or worry or longing. That's your best time to demonstrate or to come up with your original creativity.

This kind of original creativity doesn't have any set ballpark, obviously because it is not comparable to anything from the past.

A very interesting insight: Such output need not be beautiful or ideal, which our minds constantly long to seek and achieve. Conversely, an original creativity of this kind, without precedence, will be universally appreciated.

This is an incredible axiom.

11

IDENTIFY YOUR INNATE TALENT, INNER CALLING

Uncover your passion like a sculptor, chipping away the stone to reveal the masterpiece lurking beneath the surface, waiting to be released.

Understand your inner personality.

Strengthen your intellect.

You may be inspired by a larger purpose, but a well-fortified intellect is necessary to organize your activities and pursue the goal with consistency.

Are your actions selfish and self-centered, or are you truly dedicated to a higher ideal?

The higher the goal, the greater your energy, creativity, and power.

Feel at one with a larger circle of people.

Then you will feel less insecure and competitive.

You will no longer fight imaginary enemies.

Finally, understand that the world and all it has to offer are impermanent, passing, and ephemeral.

Its inherent value is zero.

The spirit, the only permanent factor in life, adds value to the world.

Seek spirit.

The world will come to you unsought.

You will achieve effortless success and happiness in the world, while you gain enlightenment.

Don't waste any more time stumbling through life.

Identify your purpose and strive to express it in your work, play, and your relationships.

Living life on purpose will translate to better well-being for you, your family, and your world.

Don't be an 'extra' in your own movie *(feature film)*

12

STOP DOING SOMETHING FOR THE SAKE OF DOING A THING

 *We have been told time and again to start doing this, that, and something or the other.*

Don't we make 'to-do' lists every day or quite often when we are in the mood to act, behave or pretend to be efficient and super smart?

The activities that are essential and needed, when you look closely get done at the right time, quite effortlessly and appropriately, as always. This may include such things as drinking water to quench thirst, carrying one's passport to travel, studying/preparing for tests of various kinds.

Instead of making a list to do more things, set goals at a macro level for your own original and real self. This may sound far too obvious and easy, yet one needs to introspect and commit to discovering one's innate and unique traits, personality, skills, needs, and individualistic characteristics. What sounds difficult is not impossible, and they are highly essential and much needed.

Put an end to the 'to-do' lists. Most importantly, learn to stop doing things that you have been doing unaware, habitually with abysmal or no beneficial outcome of any kind. Likewise, the other important thing to do consciously is to stop doing certain things regularly. Declutter your mind and life. Think of this as similar to uncluttering, throwing away old stuff from every nook and corner of your home/household. It is incredible and surprising that when it is done regularly, we are bound to get a new and better set of stuff and things that are directly complementary to our true and higher selves, giving ourselves an opportunity to get better, smarter, and go higher.

Let's not get into any matrix of mess and clutter our minds on why and how this happens per medical, psychological, or technological cause-and-effect reasons here.

At this juncture, there is no need to get into empirical studies or analysis to accept the truth that is axiomatic.

Just stop doing some of the stuff and things, periodically. Think about it. Have you ever considered evaluating certain things you have been doing? This is like the birds culling or shedding their worn-out and useless feathers, in a set pattern and time.

Make your most important things and stuff of your life a creative need, viz., breathing and quenching thirst. If what you have chosen to become is in order, aptly fit, right and smart, you'll end up doing all the essential stuff and things automatically, naturally and appropriately. If that's not happening, please resist and check on what you have been doing about yourself instead of making mindless 'to-do' lists, which you don't keep up doing anyway and which may not be essential or effective or much needed for yourself, anyway!

When we recognize, acknowledge, and stop doing certain worthless things, not only do we end up doing the worthy beautifully and joyfully, but we also become better, smarter, and go much higher.

13

WELCOME PROBLEMS, FEARS, LIMITATIONS, AND SETBACKS WITH EQUANIMITY

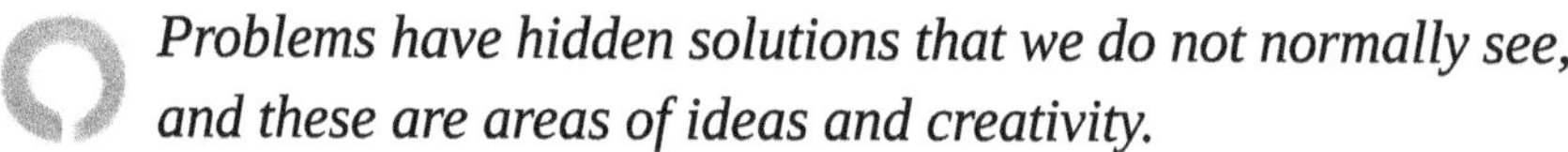 *Problems have hidden solutions that we do not normally see, and these are areas of ideas and creativity.*

More innovation, better and quicker innovations happen when you work inside your familiar world, including:

Problems, fears, limitations, setbacks, rules, and all other such things.

Use the options or possibilities carefully for new tasks and to resolve problems.

You don't have to wait for inspiration or for a special person with great ideas. You can create new and exciting things or conceive new and exciting ideas and solutions from within your own source, right inside.

Most of the choicest ideas have evolved from within ourselves at close quarters: the physical space and time immediately surrounding you have all the components and elements within your reach. But most of us waste our time and energy searching outside, looking outward and hoping to find things outside, that too with confidence, and that's an irony of fallacy. Sit back and think about it in your past in different situations and with people.

The function may follow form in certain cases, and it is certainly not always. Problems come with a solution built-in yet not easily visible, obviously. Why that is not found and figured out easily is simply because we never ever looked inside the problem. The solutions are available when the problems are clearly understood in time, place, context, persons, and situations. When it is done appropriately, you will certainly get the necessary leads to finding solutions and come up with innovations of all kinds on all accounts. It may sound like an incredible paradox, but it is practically real. You are actually better at searching for benefits and solutions from the given situational problems than in seeking from extraneous sources, arbitrarily at random—which mostly we are habituated to doing. When we find a solution from inside the given situation, it would be more original.

This idea also implies using existing resources extremely efficiently. When there are enough constraints around resources, we can prevent ideation wastage or disorder and focus productive thinking into that limited space where the creative solutions are frequently hiding. From inside might not always deliver the best solution to a given problem, but it will almost certainly provide you with the most creative one. Seeking a solution from the inside is a rich space full of surprises and creative ideas. You simply have to get used to looking for the non-obvious components and solutions inside the problem *in situ* first.

14

FALL IN LOVE WITH BOREDOM

Happiness must be ensued. It cannot be forcefully pursued. Desire or joy pursued is temporal. True bliss ensues from action. Happiness is a state. You enter when you no longer want to change your state and are satisfied with it.

The greatest threat to success is not apprehension about the future but boredom, as we have labeled many of the mundane yet essential everyday chores.

The only way to become excellent in anything is to be endlessly excited, fascinated, and ecstatic to do the same thing over and over. You have to fall in love with boredom.

Smart and successful people stick to the schedule; others let less important stuff get in the way and are busy with less important and simple pleasures of life. These may seemingly appear to be urgent and important at times, those that give temporary pleasures.

When a habit is truly important and effective, you have to stick to it as a life-saving exercise; treating it like an emergency. Find your own way to make the repetitive habits fun, interesting, or even playful. Any such self-discovery, tailor-made to your moods and environments, would take you far toward your goal, destination, or objective, smoothly and surely.

Writing, studying, working out, painting or whatever you need to do need not give you joy, pleasure or excitement all the time. But projecting the mind to the end result, the recognition, the patronage or rewards does wonders. Virtually and vividly bring it to your mind and experience the results that you are preparing yourself for. Virtual visualization does wonders, cathartic, addictive and exhilarating. And the beauty is you end up reaching your dream with your persistent habits. When we enjoy doing whatever we do with love, interest and some bravado, making the throughput, the ways and means itself become a celebration, leave alone the grand finale of realizing the target.

It's alright to be bored. Accept uncertainty. It is a signal, indicator, and suggestion to learn.

If you are having fun all the time, you won't notice that you are having fun.

So you have to be bored sometimes, accepting the complexities of life is essential to your well-being.

Absolute certainty is impossible.

Nothing is certain in life because that idea itself is your expectation as planned in your mind.

The sooner you accept that fact, it will be easier to be bored, accept the uncertainties and enjoy life.

Embrace the existential situation; you'll be able to take the appropriate steps.

15

NEGATIVE AND IRRITATING PEOPLE INSPIRE AND INDUCE US TO SUPERIOR STUFF

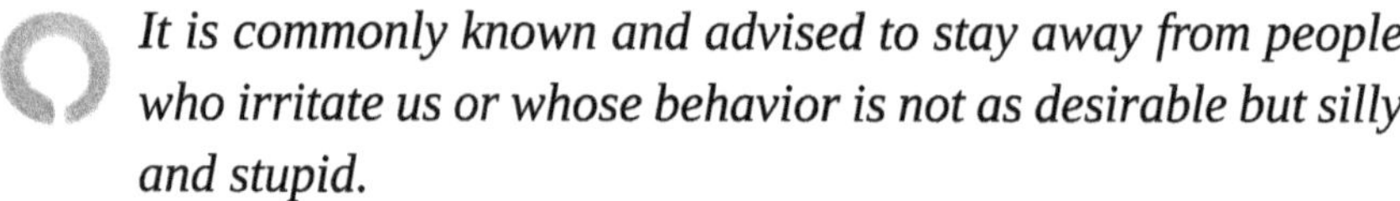 *It is commonly known and advised to stay away from people who irritate us or whose behavior is not as desirable but silly and stupid.*

The point/fact is that we are seeing those negative attributes that are hidden in us, and we are conscious of getting rid of them or abhorring them.

Once you accept this fact, whether you believe totally and are convinced or not, such encounters with certain people will not bother you. On the contrary, be thankful to them for mirroring the negative and awkward attributes you are covering up, avoiding with effort, and trying hard to get rid of!

In fact, use it as a reminder. When we consciously surrender to this, we will get a big relief and explore the world of portent potential and possibilities of the universe.

This would lead you to explore and connect with those who share your aspirational values and those who have already achieved.

In this aspect, there are immense opportunities and chances:

#1 to meet those who have achieved what you have always wanted. Obviously, this is far more effective, interesting, and useful.

#2 to study, analyze and understand this factor and factors that got the people you admire to have achieved and reached the crescendo.

Project those attributes and lessons onto your preferred goals and desires. This too, in fact, is a very interesting exponential exercise in your contemporary, day-to-day life.

Surround yourself or stay in touch with those who are complementary to your life and its desires, goals, and purpose.

Don't be eager to spend your precious time and efforts to please or seek approval from people, family, friends, or social. This is a common habit we have acquired unknowingly or in an unplanned way since our childhood. This gives us some kind of ego satisfaction, false approval, and admiration from others, which are totally useless. Think about it for a moment. All of us have been sucked into doing this unwittingly.

We all need a reason to be, and when that's strong and purposeful, we would focus our efforts to lead our lives happily every moment with no complaints. IKIGAI is a beautiful Japanese expression to give every day meaning and joy to every simple aspect of life.

Caring about something greater than yourself, especially the creatively conceptualized version as projected in our minds, is in effect superficial and of synthetic value.

When we have a reason, purpose, or desire, a special power to take action sets in to achieve/realize it. That too, you'll achieve it with ease and in a natural flow of joy, fun, and happiness. This is a common phenomenon and an aftereffect/outcome/result for anyone in tune and alignment with their true intent and purpose.

The flaw that you notice in someone you meet is probably a flaw of yours, too! If you didn't have it, you wouldn't have noticed it so easily either.

Likewise, the determination to convince someone might stem from not being completely convinced yourself of what you are trying to convince them to get over!

Avoid the routine habit of making conscious efforts to convince others. Just sit back and think about why, in the first place, you are attempting to do that or what the reason and cause are for you to do that mindless exercise?

It could be ego, wanting to demonstrate superiority, to belittle others and so on, which in effect points out that you are weak, inferior and dumb in 'that' area, *whatever that could be*!

We should be thankful to those for mirroring our negative factors that we have tried to cover up, struggling to get rid of. In fact, use it as a good and positive reminder to get rid of them.

When you consciously surrender to this, you will get a big relief and explore the world of portent potentials and possibilities.

Give yourself an opportunity to explore and connect with those who share your aspirations and values, those who have already achieved what you aspire to.

Meet with those who have achieved whatever you have always wanted. Obviously, this is far more effective, interesting, and profoundly meaningful.

Study, analyze and understand the facts and factors that enabled the people you admire to achieve and reach the crescendo.

Project those attributes and lessons onto your preferred goals and desires.

This is, in fact, a very interesting experiential exercise in your contemporary day-to-day life.

Surround yourself and stay in touch with those who are complementary to your life ambitions and its desires, goals, and 'xyz'.

16

REMOVE ALL THE *'COULD-HAVE-BEENS'*, *'WOULD-HAVE-BEENS'*, AND *'SHOULD-HAVE-BEENS'* FROM YOUR PERSONAL VOCABULARY

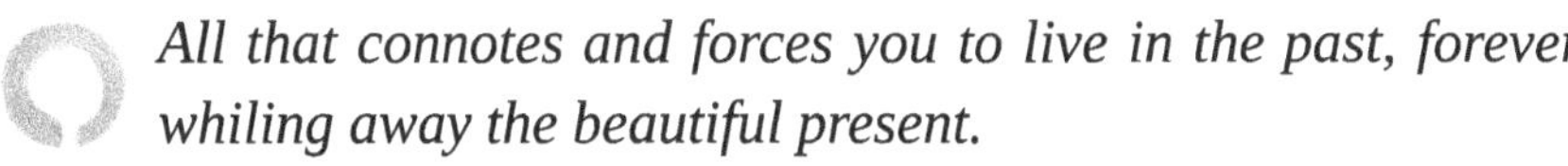 *All that connotes and forces you to live in the past, forever whiling away the beautiful present.*

Self-pity, damages your self-image for growth. Respect yourself more, aim high and be confident with total belief in yourself. Think about yourself from another standpoint: If you don't respect or believe you deserve much more and better, who else on earth would work for you to deserve the immense portent potential? What and how you think of yourselves and the world, the energy, attention and interest are directed accordingly. The net outcome or results are totally in your control and capability; a capability to have higher and true self-esteem. Bear in mind that your self-image, self-worth and your self-pity, unfortunately equally so, determine your success, wealth and destiny.

These 'IFs'-oriented stories surely may massage your ego and justify your ineptitude, giving you some sort of alibi and endorsing your self-pity. This would just empower you to be inactive, dissuading you from attending to what's at hand at this moment. This past, historic, and nostalgic bad habit is insurance against a good future.

Eliminate the past thoughts interfering with your present. This is nothing new when you hear it or read it simply on the surface. But the biggest problem is when certain select/key events or thoughts from the past 'pose' as great revelations, reasons to substantiate successes you had ignored, missed, or bypassed, and you believe in them, then the trouble starts.

Pose means: to puzzle, confuse, or baffle and that's what all these could have done; with no certainty or truth in them. Belief in these horrendous thoughts is highly dangerous; constantly colliding, interfering, fighting and seeking your attention all the time, wasting your time and efforts from the present and now.

If you keep working in the present and now, the results will show. And the world will join you.

Read the words 'keep working' again and again.

One needs to work consistently, making marginal improvements in the chosen area(s) with total commitment without seeking any gain or outcome during the process.

Have you noticed that anything that gives instant joy, pleasure, or benefit never lasts for long?

It could be tasting the best wines and whiskeys, wearing fine jewelry or owning anything new, whereas small changes and simple efforts carried out consistently and patiently lead to/contribute to remarkable results that make great contributions and positive, reliable changes.

Little do we understand or accept the fact that little improvements every day lead to lasting and phenomenal results, outcomes or outputs. Look at the way a tree grows, a river flows... In martial arts, only those who focus on the chosen aspect or a part at a given time consistently become champions; the same is the norm in other fields. It is neither possible to do two things at any given time nor is it effective to even think about something else while you are doing a thing, let alone improving.

When we make marginal enhancements to our efforts, let's say growth at about 1 percent every day that leads to over 30 times from the starting point. Art of all kinds is perfected by daily, consistent, and patient practice. Prodigies are the outcome of patient practice; the only difference being they have not allowed their minds to wander on other sundry activities for instant or temporal fun (or even results).

From your many goals and ambitions, choose one which, when accomplished, would make a big, bold and beneficial result that would make everything else almost redundant. Once the major goal is identified, jettison the lesser goals; it becomes easier to focus on the one with the desired and certain outcome. What is the one outcome with all the specifics? Then the process comes into focus, and you know that is to make tiny changes for small improvements on that single pursuit. Make meaningful progress on a daily basis; your mantra.

17

DON'T BE EAGER TO ACCEPT UNWARRANTED SOLUTIONS AND ADVICE, NOR OFFER ANY

 *Remember that no one cares about your failures (or you) as much as you do.*

People are not paying as close attention as you think to your personal failures or your "real self" anyway.

When you share your problems with your friends, you don't expect them to have the solutions. We all want to be just listened to. Have you noticed that even strangers come up with their strange solutions (and problems, of course), presumed as great and offer it to you on a platter, though you had never addressed your situation to them? This has nothing to do with you or your situation or problem; it is merely a fact that people get some sort of comfort, solace, and support when they know that others, anybody is also going through some trouble at a given time. Instead of just listening to others, they volunteer automatically with a whole load of responses, answers, and solutions. It's not that they are fair and broad-minded to listen out of empathy. No. It's just that it is highly satisfying to them, a cheap thrill which gives them relief from their troubles, worries, and apprehensions.

Likewise, when your family or friends come to you with their narratives, don't burden yourself to give solutions as you are not expected to resolve, give ideas and solutions. This does not mean you have chosen to be selfish. At the outset, in the corner of your consciousness, it might appear to be so, yet choose to be smart and stay away, totally. In fact, you will be doing them a favor besides, of course, importantly to yourself. The reason for emphasis is the simple fact that a trouble of any kind, when it is discussed with multiple people many times, grows up in multitudes, exponentially. On most instances, when a certain event is not communicated, it is as good as it had never happened in the first place. There could be exceptions to this rule, as this is not implied as a universal law.

Be convinced of the following tenets at all times:

1. People are not as interested in you and me as we had always believed or imagined.
2. Not everyone has to like you and me. After all, we do not like everyone.
3. Be brutally honest. Most of the things we do for others are in fact, for ourselves.

<u>18</u>
LEARN TO LISTEN MORE

You will be much liked and appreciated for your listening skills. But bear in mind that it is difficult to listen, irrespective of the subjects or the conversationalists, because we are built that way.

People speak 150 to 250 words per minute, whereas we can digest up to 300 to 500 words per minute.

Your ears work a little faster than your mouth. The average number of words you're able to listen to per minute is around 450.

Listening makes us impatient; makes anybody impatient, and that's why to be liked in any kind of conversation or even to be successful, let's be conscious to listen.

You may not be at work in hospitality or customer services, but it will be good to know that when the person waiting on a guest repeats the order verbatim, the guest ends up enjoying the overall services, including the quality and taste of the food being served. Of course, the added benefit for the service provider is a better tip or even a higher billing for the business as the case may be. The same is applicable in other industries. This is to emphasize that to be able to repeat, one needs to listen intently first. That's it.

Improve your empathy; have the right attitude.

A genuine interest in people, an interest in learning humility, empathy, self-awareness and emotional self-control would set you apart and take you to places of importance, giving you phenomenal importance and a special identity.

Empathetic listening is a forgotten skill. When you leave the cocooned existence you call your home, you are suddenly exposed to a raft of new sights, smells, tastes, POVs (points of view), and sufferings. You will start accepting things and others, which obviously enhances your empathy and listening.

To improve your empathy and perfect your listening skills, put yourself into unfamiliar situations where you have neither mastery nor control. The incredible truth is that one need not have mastery or expertise in any of the specific subjects or technology to be liked, appreciated, and win accolades. But first, learn to listen more.

19

QUESTION, QUESTION, AND QUESTION YOURSELF

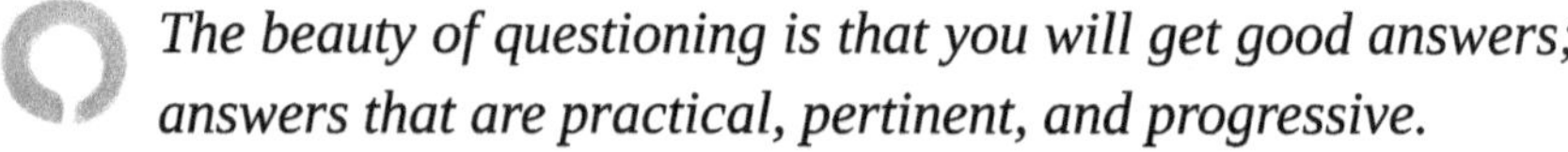 *The beauty of questioning is that you will get good answers; answers that are practical, pertinent, and progressive.*

Questioning can be used to establish the premises or the base through stringent analysis. This is a disciplined questioning process, used to establish truths, reveal underlying assumptions, and separate knowledge from ignorance.

Why do I think this? What exactly do I think? > Clarifies your thinking and explains the origins of your ideas

How do I know this is true? What if I thought the opposite? > challenges assumptions

How can I back this up? What are the sources? > Look for evidence

What might others think? How do I know I am correct? > Considers alternative perspectives

What if I am wrong? What are the consequences if I am? > Examines consequences and implications

Why did I think that? Was I correct? What conclusions can I draw from the reasoning process? > Questions the original questions.

This process prevents you from relying on hearsay and limits strong emotional responses. This process helps you build something that lasts.

And so question all the original questions for all the right answers.

20
BEWARE OF DEFAULT HABITS

The incredible truth about habits, however marginal, insignificant, small, low, minor, slight, minimal or negligible it may appear at a given time, its portent potential and its compounding effects are phenomenal. There's no doubt. Tiny, nearly imperceptible changes you make in your habits can make a huge difference over time.

Habits and **mental disciplines** are invaluable investments, offer enormous opportunities and allow you to grow for the rest of your life. More importantly, they allow you to stand out from the crowd, making you unique and distinguishable, ending up where you truly desire and deserve.

Here's the simple truth: This works either way, make the necessary changes for improvement consistently in your areas of innate skills and interests for assured success and joy. What starts as small grows into something much bigger. Or, by default, you postpone or settle for instant glory and gratification for petty pleasure and pay a price that's unaffordable. Secondly, it may also be too late to make corrections as the damage you have chosen to cause is irreparable.

Habits are nothing but the compound interest of self-improvement and mental discipline. In the same way that money multiplies, the effects of your habits, good and bad, multiply as you repeat them. They may seem to make very little difference on any given day and are easy to ignore, but the impact they deliver over time is enormous. Just wait for a couple of years or even months to see the value, every which way.

Make small choices and changes in your diet, exercise or money savings... It's true, it may not seem to matter much in the moment. Human tendency is to ignore all the simple changes and their synonyms. Get over that silly habit of embracing your default habits, first. Small decisions don't matter all that much on any given day independently. However, as days turn to weeks and weeks to months and months to years, those tiny choices compound. Please understand.

Out of sheer habit, it's easier to just live in the moment and make a decision in a jiffy for instant pleasure or limited benefits.

We are tuned to choose the easier path in the moment and do whatever we want for instant pleasure. This could be due to selfishness, ego, habit, or even living for others. In fact, our choice of decisions and habits ought to be from us for us. This sounds simple and easy, but you have to learn to invest time and more in yourself. Most importantly, get into the mindset of simple improvements of your USP and distinctive capabilities and make them your main, primary, and one goal.

When we repeat the simple, silly, cute and tiny **errors** day after day, replicating poor decisions, duplicating tiny mistakes, and rationalizing little excuses, our small wrong and bad choices lead to disastrous doldrums. The problem is we don't even know we have wrong habits and are doing vague things, oblivious to our true 'self' or its real needs. That itself is our bad habit.

Always question your default habits.

21
APPEAL TO EMOTION AND EXPERIENCE

 *They are more powerful than appealing to reason or logic.*

Negative emotions can be a threat to wise decision-making.

Before 'acting', there is a feeling that motivates you to act, the craving. Feelings come both before and after the behavior. How we feel influences how we act, and how we act influences how we feel.

Pleasure and satisfaction sustain behavior. Feeling motivated gets you to act. Feeling successful gets you to repeat.

The reward for a good habit or trait is the habit itself, and it needs to be enjoyable for it to last.

What comes to you easily or rather relatively better, faster and more easily than for the majority of people?

You need not necessarily be born with a rare set of abilities to find peace, success, or happiness.

Any work you tend to do happily is the one in which you are not just likely to but certainly achieve greatness.

You can also win by being different.

Create your own 'stuff': anything based on what comes to you simply, easily, and spontaneously.

Choose to create your own narrow category or area of expertise.

Transform the odds (against you) to ones where they are in your favor.

Fulfill your own potential. Stop comparing, complaining, criticizing, convincing, and competing.

Your limitations or certain capabilities should not be allowed to define and hold you back from realizing your higher purpose, value, and _ _ _ _ _

Your behaviors should align with your personality and skills, however you rate them to be. Your self-evaluation by itself is redundant and limiting. Enhance more of it and faster on the things that come easy. You are special with 'that'.

Choose your right field of life's activities that has lesser or no competition.

Learn to handle the boredom of doing every day, doing your 'stuff' over and over again...

You are good at that which comes to you easily like your signature. Do you make efforts, plan, and think before you sign?

Feeling motivated gets you to act. Feeling successful gets you to repeat. Satisfaction = liking minus wanting.

Being poor is not having too little, it is wanting more and more of things that are popularly accepted as the 'in' thing by others. Conversely, you should fulfill your innate needs only with complementary things.

How you process feelings has a connection to your happiness and productivity.

(Don't put too much weight or emphasis on the problems but on solutions and options)

22

CONNECT, CONNECT, AND CONNECT

- — What you love
- — Whatever you're good at
- — What you can be paid for
- — What the world needs.

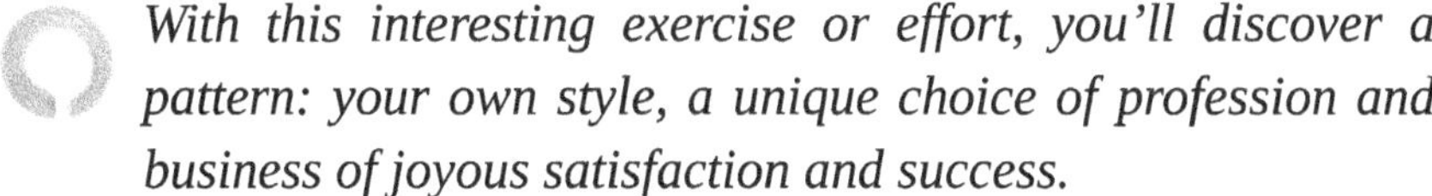

With this interesting exercise or effort, you'll discover a pattern: your own style, a unique choice of profession and business of joyous satisfaction and success.

The key is discovering yourself and the things you like and dislike most.

Ask yourself: Is this the most important activity that needs my total attention right now?

Interesting things would start happening when you start pursuing what you love.

Don't be hijacked by other people's ideas, opinions, advice, and views.

Start giving yourself more importance. For this, you have to learn to CONNECT with yourself, your true self.

It may sound incredible, impossible, and improbable.

But then, that's how and, importantly, what led the millions of millionaires to their banks.

What do you want?

Set the goal big: Connect to something audacious and strong with a holistic purpose.

What do you stand for?

What do you love?

How much time do you spend doing what you love?

You should know what you want and do.

Do you really know **what** you **want**?

Give your imagination an opportunity.

Make up your mind in true relevance to yourself.

You'll never be happy or successful pursuing other people's expectations.

What do you want to **learn**?

Have you ever spent any time figuring it out?

What you learn should clearly connect with your innate needs, talents, and mindset.

When you learn thoughtfully and aptly, you will do whatever you have chosen to do with so much ease and enjoyment that you won't notice the passing time while achieving more.

Block everything else out and focus intensely on the one BIG goal. Focus on extreme output, productivity, and creativity.

Change your environment, peer group, your daily routine behaviors, and your identity.

New 'avatar' for the new businesses or targets in the new entity.

For every new goal you set, you need a new identity and vice versa.

You need to clearly identify the key activities that will produce your desired outcome.

Label yourself to achieve your goal. What does that mean? Give yourself the right label right now for what you have chosen to become later.

It could be anything: Actor, Writer, Artist, Scientist, Global Leader, Businessperson of x or y.

Our successes have to do with focusing on our core desires, which unleashes our conquering force. Desire, per se, is ambiguously referred to as a bad, wrong, and negative quality.

Learning how to unleash and use your conquering force, that crucial ingredient, is vital to your success in anything: making money, improving relationships, boosting self-esteem, and gaining confidence. It all comes from the amazing conquering force within each of us, powered by our desires.

Once you destroy the invisible obstacles such as fear, self-doubt, lack of self-esteem, wrong paradigms, beliefs, wrong opinions and fear of failure, you will be able to access the outcome of all your desires. Your obstacles stem from your past limiting beliefs. These are the beliefs that cause you to interpret the situation as an obstacle; being the result of limiting beliefs.

23

INTELLIGENT EXCUSES ARE TRUE LIES

Don't ever make excuses and dwell in self-pity.

When you do that, you are ineffective and less productive and end up choosing your ineptness, laziness, or weakness as your personality. That's, in fact, not you. You deserve much more and better than that.

Doubts, uncertainty, makeovers, and make-ups are all true lies.

External pressure and imagined perceptions of potential losses force your focus on all the things that could go wrong in your world. We need to be wary of this trick of our minds.

Your mindset tends to shift away from all of the potential good things around to the problems. It is natural, so tread consciously with care, attention, and confidence.

You are wired to avoid unpleasant things but progress, benefit or victory is in your ability to take on unpleasant things more often and of higher magnitude with the right spirits. This may sound incredible, bitter and even preposterous. There is no escape to it in any field. Don't allow your mind to wallow in creating excuses and justifications of a smart order. **Any excuse, reasoning or justification is an absolute lie.**

NATURE is not put together by thought, as religion is, as belief is, or dogmas, sects, and more. Stay away from anything that's not natural nor evolved naturally.

Think, Work, and do from within, in a natural way—your natural way in alignment with true intentions for definitive outcomes. You do that consistently with a sustainable way and commitment to seeing the outcome evolve so simply—in a studied nonchalance.

Doubts, Intelligent Excuses, Justifications, Makeovers and Make-ups are all true lies.

<u>24</u>

STOP FINDING SOLUTIONS
TO ANXIETY

They are your invention and imagination.

Don't be troubled by worries that have not yet happened, nor do you know anything about them. And don't waste your time finding solutions to something that doesn't exist.

Lots of people are perpetually worried for no reason.

Haven't we known so many who were worried in the name of being responsible, moral, or straightforward?

Such people give away unwarranted and unlimited advice, opinions, and views until they die.

The incredible truth is that they have died without knowing what they were worried about all along.

No need to worry about anxieties, which are intangible and unreal.

25

STOP LIVING IN AN EXTERNAL WORLD

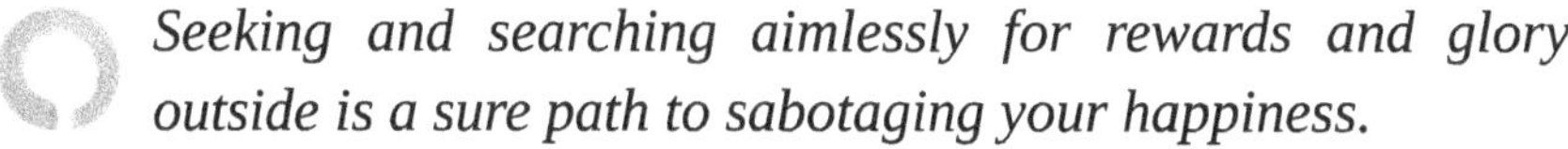 *Seeking and searching aimlessly for rewards and glory outside is a sure path to sabotaging your happiness.*

Live inside yourself: *Discover, Connect,* and *believe* in yourself to find greatness.

Go inside.

Become your best at what you are capable of and that which comes to you so naturally.

Identify your true, innate, and characteristic factors.

Develop that all the time, sustain it, and discover the immense treasure and storehouse within you.

Do your best to do what you can.

There's no point in envying someone else who has been successful, nor does it do any good to constantly complain about your lack of opportunities.

Simply work on what comes to you naturally and do it well.

And fortune will surely come your way.

Always make an effort, no matter the circumstances or situation, to bring out your true self—your inner protagonist, the champion who can deal with whatever you may ever face.

This way, all of us will be able to encounter truth and discover bliss.

26

DON'T CHOOSE TO BE RIGHT

Focus on being productive, happy, and humble instead of being busy, 'proving' right.

There's no such thing as absolute right or wrong.

People tend to choose to be right in arguments, deliberations, and even petty fights. They even go to the extent of validating themselves to be right with inordinate time expended, taking a whole load of effort.

Instead, they should focus on happiness and well-being for everyone.

It is grossly wrong to presume that their level of happiness would come down drastically in proportion to the increase in others' happiness. In reality, it doesn't work like that.

The time and effort wasted are much more than what would have taken to achieve whatever one needed in the name of their pride, personal goal, or need instead.

Even if you feel right in a given situation, circumstance in a particular environment, stop proving yourself right. This simple stoppage would benefit you enormously on several accounts.

When you don't attach yourself to being right, it would significantly improve your decision-making and make you smarter.

Replace the joy of being right with the joy of learning what is true and choosing to be happy instead.

27
DON'T EVER POSTPONE HAPPINESS

You could be happy anytime, even right now. If not now, when? So, be happy.

Postponing happiness is a mindless and meaningless exercise that most of us do habitually out of sheer ignorance.

Your happiness is not to be subjected as a consequence of extraneous events and persons. Your happiness is entirely dependent on your mindset, and, in fact, it is well within your means. Postponing happiness is equivalent to shying away from the present and anxiously awaiting the imagined wish, event, or wants to materialize in the distant future, without even knowing why and what exactly is the reason for postponing. Anyway, it is not possible to be certain about the future, so why waste the present time whiling away with anxiety, apprehension, fear, or doubt. Plan with your own purpose and set of priorities, which are certainly needed and highly appreciated. But learn to celebrate the present with whatever, whoever, and wherever, instead. For all you know, this itself, would prepare you to reap the benefits of the imagined and desired happiness. Just for the sake of worrying about the unknown future, you don't need to ruin the beautiful present meant to be enjoyed happily now.

28

MAKE 'DOING IT NOW,' YOUR MOTTO

Anything that's kept pending for any time period, however long or short, would trouble us forever.

The main reason for a thing kept undone by most people is the intention to want to do it better, beautifully, and correctly at a later time. This is a big blunder. Instead, just do it right now or rather as soon as possible. Don't wait for an ideal time or a bright spark or a smart person or a great environment to work or to complete a task to get the benefits. By postponing (indefinitely), you are not going to achieve anything - let alone do it better. Any postponement is your mind's uncertainty, laziness, and an excuse for inaction. It could also be the increasing difficulty of adapting to new thoughts for eventual action, which always confronts all of us in all ways.

Too much of 'thinking' in the name of special planning for a greater deed in the future is no good, not worthwhile because it generates bad ideas and ideas that are irrelevant to you. Let go of such thoughts.

To get rid of uncertainty, get comfortable with the unknown. Exploring uncertain terrains gives you an opportunity to learn and experience new and beautiful aspects in life. Moreover, it drives away boredom, keeps you from routine habits, and even elixirs and substances of any kind. Instead, learn to do it now. **Make 'doing it now' your motto.**

29

LIFE IS NOT BASED ON YOUR OR ANYONE'S BELIEF

 *It's based on your experiences, happenings, and nature's bounty.*

Never believe anyone's words when they come from someone without real-life experiences on the given subject. It is common across the world for people to give instant and expert opinions about worldly matters or, for example, about whatever you intend to do. If the person happens to be in a notable position in terms of official rank, attached to a renowned business, or enjoying an inherited socio-economic lifestyle, they will speak their minds out with their beliefs of all kinds: projected thoughts, imagined situations, or guesswork, while solving your life's queries with their superficial belief systems. Be careful; partially the mistake is, in fact, ours! Yes, we don't need to believe in the advice, suggestions, and opinions based on someone's beliefs just because he or she is rich or famous due to varied factors. Instead, believe in yourself, your beliefs, and you will do well to go to a specialist in the given field of your need.

How could you take someone's opinion, conviction, faith, or a thing believed and accepted by more individuals as true?

Any doctrine, ideology, dogma, tenet, view, theory, impression, assessment, notion, point of view or sentiment is a belief; a blind belief. It could become a superstition when any of these is taken literally, seriously and practically. Historically, it has been the case or tactic utilized by cunningly smart people to wield, command and control over others. Instead, let's go our own ways, experience it totally to carry on with our lives. It is impossible to know what it takes and how to learn to become perfect in any field just depending on others' beliefs.

Let's learn to believe in ourselves with our own ways and means, practically.

Belief, by itself, is a word that ought to be understood, **belief, credence, credit, faith.**

These nouns denote mental acceptance of the truth, actuality, or validity of something:

1. A principle, proposition, idea, etc., accepted as true
2. Opinion; conviction without need for proof or evidence

(Or mental picture of) the future

An irrational belief arising from ignorance or fear

Belief - a vague idea in which some confidence is placed;

1. Absolute certainty in the trustworthiness of another: **Confidence, dependence, faith, reliance, trust.**

2. Mental acceptance of the truth or actuality of something: **Credence, credit, faith.**

3. Something believed or accepted as true by a person: **Conviction, feeling, idea, mind, notion, opinion, persuasion, position, sentiment, view.**
   Presumption

30

DON'T BE OBSESSED WITH WHAT YOU WANT AND 'THAT' YOU DON'T HAVE

When 'what' you want and what you don't have occupied your mind most of the time, you are preventing or stopping that which you need the most from reaching you.

Our mind is preoccupied with useless thoughts, and that prevents us from realizing what we deserve and desire.

Be wary of the incredible fact that 80% of our thoughts are totally negative and 95% of them are repetitive.

Don't worry and sweat it out hard. There are ways and means to escape from this rut, bad habit, and perspective.

Rediscover the joy in your hobbies, whatever that may be. Meditation is of enormous help and with some guidance in the early stages to get initiated, anyone could enjoy the present moment joyfully and productively. Fill your life with new experiences, meeting new people and visiting new places. None of these needs to cost a lot of money and major effort. Make this a deliberate practice, i.e., to fill your life with new experiences. You will be amazed at the effects and results.

31

WE DON'T HAVE TO AGREE ON EVERYTHING WITH EVERYBODY

People could be emotional about certain issues and have particular opinions, but there is hope and possibility in this world and our lives. It's a matter of how we approach and handle things for the common good.

Disagreement does not mean disorder or disaster.

Disagree with or withdraw from a negotiation or discussion, yet commit to the desired outcome for mutual benefits.

PROGRESS IS YOUR PERSONAL PREROGATIVE

Material Progress versus Personal Progress.

They are different but both have to be understood as they play a contributory, collaborating, and complementary role in our life.

Having more stuff and better stuff is not real progress.

What is more important is progress, the personal progress: transforming oneself into the best that one can be. You can measure that in a number of ways. Are we happier now than we were in the past? Do we have more fulfilling lives now? Is there a definitive purpose or goal to go after? Are we mindful and conscious of our thoughts and actions at any given time? If you are, then life becomes bliss, staying in the present and not missing what is not available. Don't think of this as some spiritual stuff and don't tell yourself you are not ready for it yet.

What's sad is that most conversations these days end up quickly in loud arguments or 'shouting matches'; each one trying to prove to be right. Instead, they should choose to be happy. You don't need to be right to be happy, and if that's important or the case, then your happiness is entirely dependent on others, those you need to prove yourself to be right with conscious efforts to stay happy.

Making people think more effectively and having conversations to move forward (together) is a smarter and more peaceful way of making progress effectively. In this regard, referring to GDP, economic growth, turnover, or the rate of increase in trade of any kind is going to mislead the real human and individual progress. Because we are habituated to looking at tables, factors, and numbers - all of which are extraneous and imposed upon us or forced into our minds with some theory or another, formula, and methods. Changing this mindset may sound difficult and unacceptable, as it is ingrained by force for a long, long time.

Yes, there's an ongoing tension between material and personal progress. Please understand that without the realization of personal understanding, peace, and personal progress, no amount of material progress would satisfy us. Only when we resolve the conflict between material and personal improvements, the idea of progress could/will be realized. Your life progress becomes your choice and well within your means at your disposal.

32
AVOID SEEKING CERTAINTY

<u>33</u>

JUST TO BE YOURSELF IS
A BLESSING; BLISSFUL

Be happy.

No need to wait for reasons; several reasons will come along, but let go, allowing them to pass by.

Even if they don't, just be happy.

34

EXPECTATIONS, ROSY PROSPECTS AND POSSIBILITIES

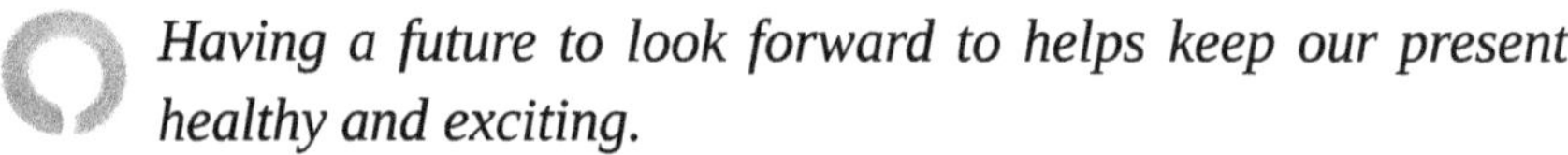 *Having a future to look forward to helps keep our present healthy and exciting.*

Anticipating something pleasurable in the future can help you get through present hardships and loneliness.

We all use this as a psychological strategy from time to time, whether or not we realize it or not.

When present reality disappoints or depresses us, we turn to planning for a more exciting future.

And so, we anticipate the lunch break through a morning of hard work, or the evening watching our favorite TV show, or catching up with friends once a week.

Planning and anticipation of a holiday gives one almost as much pleasure as the holiday itself. Sometimes, even more.

Strategizing to have something interesting and rewarding to look forward to can help you get through not just hardships and days of anxiety, but also pep up the tedium of daily existence.

So, are we saying that life minus desires and dreams with nothing to look forward to is a dull and monotonous life? Yes, I am afraid so. A life without purpose, with nothing to plan for or look forward to, is certainly not meant for humans. I can live with moments of 'just being' and 'existing' in the present, floating on a no-goal cloud -but a lifetime of it is mindless and impossible!

A healthy amount of anticipation and dreaming is, to me, a necessary element of a life well-lived and loved.

Such hope and looking forward to it are very important. Trouble arises when you allow the hope to take up a large chunk of your present time. It is then that hope sets itself on the path of hopelessness.

The trick is to anticipate little doses of future happiness planned as rewards for the big focus we give to our present moments.

35

DO NOT ANTICIPATE TROUBLE
OR WORRY ABOUT WHAT
MAY NEVER HAPPEN

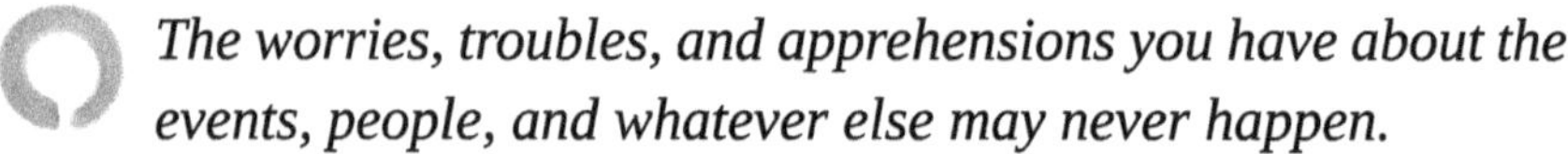 *The worries, troubles, and apprehensions you have about the events, people, and whatever else may never happen.*

According to studies, about 96% of such events do not ever happen.

Stop wasting your time and energy thinking about it.

Please understand that when your thoughts and behavior are preoccupied with imaginary troubles, you may not be ready to receive, realize, and enjoy the abundance in life.

Change your thoughts to love, kindness, peace and joy, and you'll attract more of the same.

36

BEWARE OF YOUR ENVIRONMENT. THE PEOPLE IN YOUR ENVIRONMENT ARE A MAJOR CAUSE FOR HAPPINESS

In an environment where the people are neither poor nor rich, it's very easy to make that bunch of people happy.

When people share a common goal with a projected reality, shared values, and work together, they are constantly content, happy, and more productive.

A common trust occurs and evolves in the process. This also means meaningful relationships with unconditional support.

Surround yourself with interesting people, those who are positive, supportive and would make you feel good.

<u>37</u>

PRACTICE GRATITUDE REGULARLY. YOU WILL BE AMAZED

Practice gratitude regularly by writing a journal and meditating on all the good things in your life.

Find ways to show appreciation to those close to you.

This in turn would do you a whole load of good.

Compassion and gratitude do wonders.

Try being grateful for one thing a day. You are going to be amazed at the results.

This simple aspect overcomes anger, changes your behavior, your perspective, and sets right your relationships as well.

Your highest priority-warranting actions for activities ought to be limited to a few, any day.

38

CHALLENGE YOUR MIND WITH NEW, UNKNOWN TASKS AND MULTISENSORY EXPERIENCES

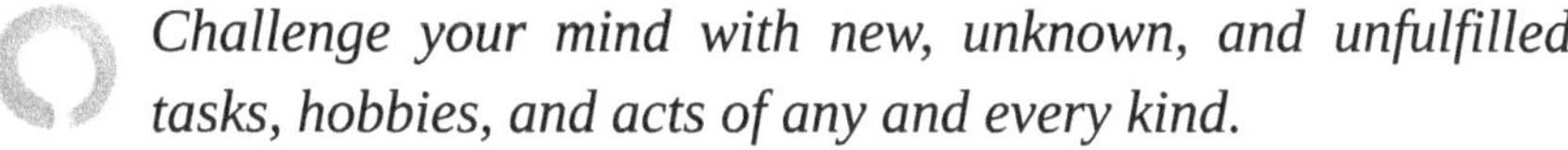 *Challenge your mind with new, unknown, and unfulfilled tasks, hobbies, and acts of any and every kind.*

Every little progress in any of these leads to happiness. It's incredible but true.

Stay busy with hobbies and activities of any kind that complement you.

Performing hobbies that you used to enjoy in different environments is yet another way to find happiness again.

You'll be able to achieve much more when you put your mind to new challenges.

39

TRY TO THINK WITHOUT WORDS

 *Master your mindset.*

Stay clear of limiting beliefs.

Try to think without words! Words are the culprits for inculcating your limiting beliefs.

Yes, it is possible.

When you do that, you end up arresting thoughts and enjoying the beautiful and supreme bliss of the NOW.

In the now, you will connect with your purpose and goal and spontaneously/automatically do what it takes to make a big difference.

The difference could be transformative, transcendent, or innovative, all for the benefit of others in your concern and interest.

It's going to be a natural flow in almost and obviously an automatic way.

Try thinking about your beautiful world without words. Don't belittle or stifle yourself with limiting beliefs or complex theories and hide behind the general excuse that this sounds incredible, preposterous, and too profound for the ordinary self—such as yourself!

This is a terrible mistake acquired over a period of time from the past from all sources of extraneous elements, factors, and people.

When you are able to stay in the present without words, you will also experience the joy and bliss of the present.

Some ways and means to stop or reduce using redundant words are interesting activities like *Koan, Haiku,*your favorite hobbies and such.

Koan is a paradoxical anecdote or riddle without a solution, used in Zen Buddhism to demonstrate the inadequacy of logical reasoning and provoke enlightenment.

A characteristic **example** of the style is the well-known **koan**: "When both hands are clapped, a sound is produced; listen to the sound of one hand clapping."

Contemplate over Koans:

- It's all nothing but Just Bits.
  - Perfection is Normal.

- There Is Want in the Midst of Plenty.
- Processing Is Power.
- More of the Same Can Be a Whole New Thing.
- Nothing Goes Away.
- Bits Move Faster Than Thought.

HAIKU: a Japanese verse form, rendered in English as three unrhymed lines of 5, 7, and 5 syllables respectively (total 17 syllables), often on some subject in nature

- Traditional writers of haiku have focused on expressing emotionally suggestive moments of insight into natural phenomena. The **purpose of haiku** is to share a brief moment or event so that the reader can bring to life in his or her mind (and thus experience the same feelings) without having to physically experience what the author is expressing in the poem.

'A World of Dew' by Kobayashi Issa

A world of dew,
And within every dewdrop.
A world of struggle.

Let go of thoughts. Too much thinking is not worthwhile because it comes up with bad ideas that are irrelevant to you and useless to anyone.

Let go of thoughts. Yes, it is repeated to emphasize.

<u>40</u>
FALL IN LOVE WITH UNCERTAINTY

Get comfortable with the unknown. Exploring uncertainties gives you an opportunity to learn and experience new, wonderful opportunities in life, in this world.

You will be pleased to know that this would drive away boredom, keep you away from routine habits, also known as bad habits, and even from the bad company of people.

41

STOP BLAMING OTHERS

For anything.

Just by blaming, you can't stop or prevent what you don't like.

Blame, again, is either directed toward the past or is a by-product in your mind from the past.

Stay away from the past.

If there's anything that differentiates a winner from losers, it is the attitude and demeanor with which whatever task is faced.

Letting go of your blaming behavior is the key to feeling happy and bringing forth opportunity and fortune in the here and now.

<u>42</u>

THE OTHER YOU IS THE REAL HERO OR PROTAGONIST IN YOU

There is another you inside you, which is the real you.

This version of you is freer than the self you think you know and rich with portent potential.

It is your essential self within yourself, where your true protagonist lives in which you are your real master.

Do your best to awaken this other self with boundless potential.

43

DON'T PUT OFF WHAT YOU CAN DO TODAY

 *You cannot regret the future.*

Avoid regretting

In fact, lead your life in such a way that the expression 'REGRET' is deleted from your mind's vocabulary.

44

DISCONNECT FROM THIS CRAZY WORLD, FREQUENTLY

Reconnect with your inner child, the real you.

You can dream big if you put your mind, passion, and devotion toward what you love and are innately capable of.

Believe in your true nature.

You have to believe in yourself first and foremost and do what you love.

You have to immerse yourself in only what inspires you to be better.

If you put enough hard work and passion into whatever you do best, you are destined for happiness and success.

<u>45</u>

LEARN, LEARN, LEARN

Learning improves your health and sleep.

It broadens your view with a broad perspective when approaching problems from a brand-new angle.

When you stop trying to better yourself and learn new things, you stop striving for goals and risk stagnating.

<u>46</u>

DIFFICULTY IS YET ANOTHER IDEA AND INVENTION OF YOUR MIND

 *You are giving dimensions to it with great elaboration.*

A big blunder

It disappears when you confront and approach to find what caused that idea in your mind and to be perceived as DIFFICULT.

Certain tasks, areas, or aspects may not be meant for you—your special, innate, true self.

Simply withdraw yourself from that which you have labeled as DIFFICULT.

Instead, strive to achieve the things for which you are, in fact, highly capable.

47

CONNECT WITH YOUR TRUE SELF, EVEN EFFORTLESS ACTIVITIES LEAD TO GREAT RESULTS

To identify that practice, practice and practice.

Practice empowers you to become effortless and effective in any given activity.

In Martial Arts' dictum, 'a lifetime of training for just that one moment (of seconds)' makes a great difference.

How you perceive life is how you will process it.

Do divergent thinking, generate new ideas, seeking solutions to problems that have persisted in your mind.

This would also help you to be patient and persistent in the present.

The more lateral activities and thinking you do, the more fired up and better off you will be.

When you are connected to your deeper infinite self, you will be confident to do the right things.

What's right, relevant or appropriate need not be rich, famous, luxurious or complicated but authentic.

Meditation and other simple methods help you to connect with yourself.

We possess within us everything we need right from the beginning.

Life's meaning or purpose is not about seeking answers from the outside nor acquiring things, most of which are unaffordable and unnecessary.

It's about looking inside.

When you encounter your pure and true self, it is a beautiful revelation of eternal bliss.

<u>48</u>

BE WILLING TO BE MISUNDERSTOOD

▪ ▪ ▪

Nothing wrong in that.

After all, you have misunderstood so many people and things for so long.

Let others misunderstand you rightly, for rightful reasons. No harm in it. At least, stop worrying about it.

49

FOR A CHANGE, THINK ABOUT YOUR BODY AND NOT YOUR WORK

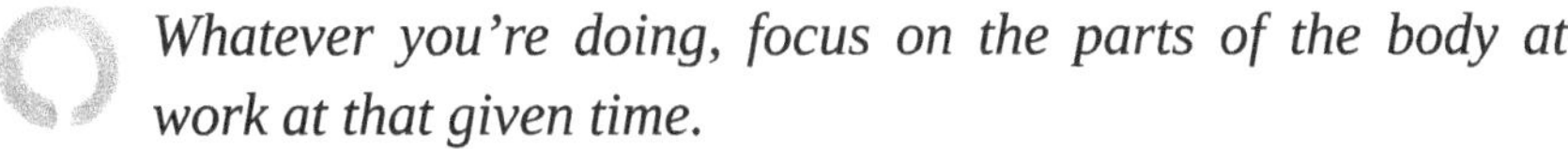 *Whatever you're doing, focus on the parts of the body at work at that given time.*

Avoid thinking about any other task, work, problem, anxiety, money, and myriad other things.

This is better than a lovely body massage.

Because this gives you an opportunity to rediscover and connect with your mind, and the real you.

50

DEFINE HAPPINESS ON YOUR ACCORD

 *Naming things properly is very important to start with.*

Expectation is a powerful attribute.

If you long for and focus on bubbling ecstasy, life may seem to disappear all the time.

Instead, acknowledge problems with a solution focused mind and be present during every small moment.

Refuse to dramatize any single emotion or feeling with wild stories and you will be able to deal with all manner of feelings and experiences.

It's your life.

It's your choice, either to suppress or overreact to your own emotions.

<h1 style="text-align:center"><u>51</u></h1>

BE MINDFUL OF THE MOMENT

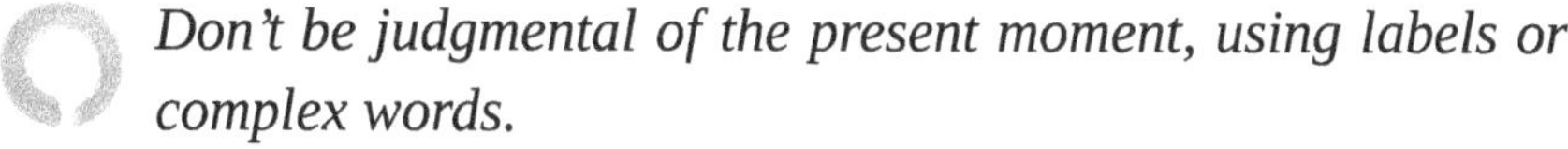 *Don't be judgmental of the present moment, using labels or complex words.*

Instead, be aware and mindful of accepting things you cannot change to enjoy a multitude of life aspects in many ways.

This helps you trust in your experiences and encourages authentic living, with a plethora of experiences and emotions of your own choice that you cherish.

52

GREEDY AMBITION COULD LEAD TO BURNOUT AND MADNESS

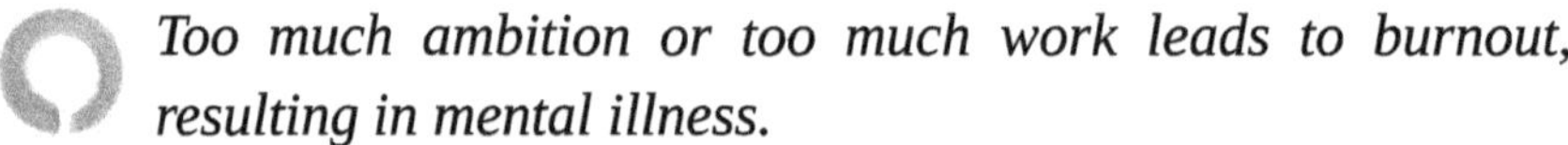 *Too much ambition or too much work leads to burnout, resulting in mental illness.*

And it doesn't matter how profitable, fun, or exciting that work, activity, or goal feels initially.

It's just a craze for novel or fashionable stuff.

Think in terms of a growth perspective as opposed to a fixed mental state or habitual mind-set; a bad behavior.

53
JUST BE WHO YOU ARE

This may seem difficult to do at the outset.

Because we all want to hide our weaknesses and portray ourselves as much more or better than we are.

Learn to be 'just who you are', knowing that it can heal your weary mind and revitalize your spirits.

But when you are true to yourself, life becomes beautiful.

54

CHANGING YOUR ATTITUDE
CHANGES YOUR LIFE

Even if you can't change your fate, you can be happy by changing your attitude toward life.

Cultivate a sense of awe and gratitude. You will be surprised on its effect and outcome.

In addition, when you connect with your inner self, the divine power, you are driven to make a positive impact on the world.

Fix a higher ideal and work with like-minded people.

55

ANOTHER ASPECT OF IMPORT FOR YOUR LIFE: DOING WHAT IS APPROPRIATE

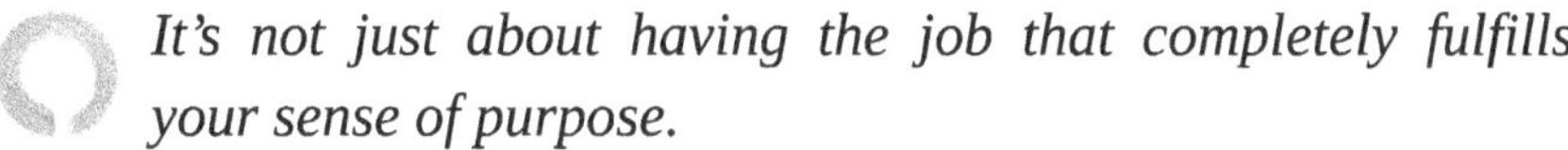 *It's not just about having the job that completely fulfills your sense of purpose.*

It's about creating a life situation that allows you to do other things that are important to you.

Have a clear picture of what you do want, as otherwise you'd make decisions that don't serve you nor would give you happiness, satisfaction, or fulfillment.

Create clear boundaries and guidelines for what's most important to you.

The rest are not suited to you.

Give importance and priority to your own priorities.

What isn't working for you in your life be it career, hobby, people, or whatever?

Understanding that would do you good.

If certain things aren't working well in your favor, it doesn't mean anything is wrong with you.

Make a list of things that don't work and what hasn't worked well.

This would give you a very good idea and clarity on what's going to work beautifully for you.

That's why it's important to' know' yourself, your core capabilities, values, and so on. When you work mindfully and pursue your natural purpose or goal, life becomes happier and more successful.

56

DO YOUR UNIQUE CHOICE OF STUFFS WITHOUT DOUBT AND FEAR

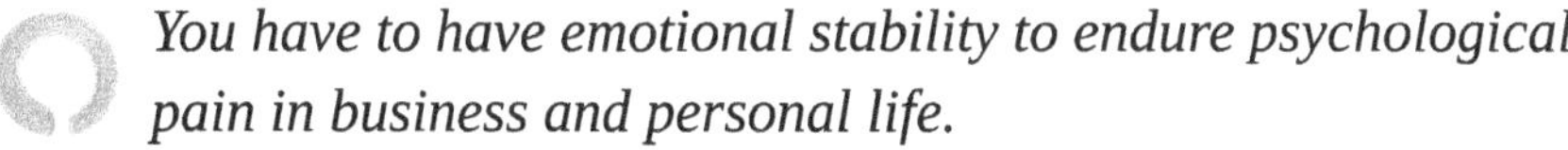 *You have to have emotional stability to endure psychological pain in business and personal life.*

You should do anything only if you have thought of something that is really unique, original and extraordinary on your own, natural accord. Comparing and competing in any way is not only a tough way to be successful but disastrous and shameful.

57

BE CURIOUS ABOUT CURIOSITY AND CONVERSATIONS

Be curious about the importance of curiosity conversations

Have conversations with people from across industries, varied backgrounds, meeting new people constantly to learn something that will broaden your mind and alter your understanding of the world.

58

MAKE EFFORTS TO REALIZE YOUR TRUE SELF

Body Mind Thoughts Action Results...

Developing a positive mindset is as much about your body as it is about your brain and mind.

Yoga and any of martial arts practices would prepare you to realize your true self.

<u>59</u>

CHALLENGES, TROUBLES, BAD LUCK…

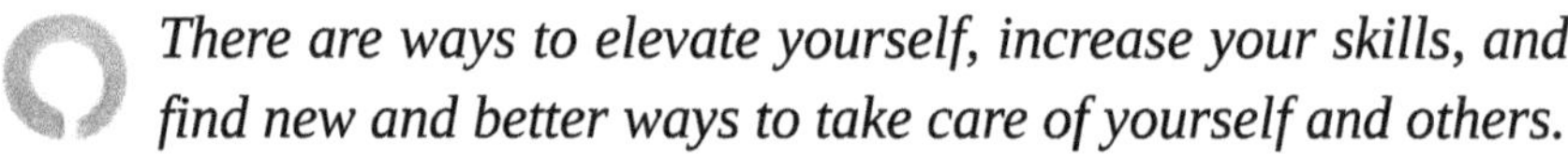 *There are ways to elevate yourself, increase your skills, and find new and better ways to take care of yourself and others.*

Welcome challenges wholeheartedly and enjoy confronting them because that is the best and the only way.

Don't ever suppress the issues or ignore the existence of these beautiful challenges, troubles, and bad luck that, in fact, would give you excellent opportunities to grow.

<u>60</u>

WE LIVE IN A VISUAL WORLD

Our world is completely visual.

Make a visual image, a collage for your life's ultimate in every key aspect. The very act of making it and viewing them often would work wonders in your life viz.:

- What would you like to DO?
- BE.
- SHARE.
- REALIZE.
- The kind of PEOPLE & ENVIRONMENT you want to be with,
- Where would you like to TRAVEL and LIVE?

This would do incredible wonders in your life to realize them all. All of us live in a visual world. Even your memory is totally visual. Think about your last vacation and the best things you have done and experienced. Just for a few moments, please close your eyes and think intently. You would remember the streets, the restaurants or bars you had visited and so on. You couldn't have remembered the taste of the wine or whiskey or food you had enjoyed nor the smell of a great cup of cappuccino.

An average person has up to about 60,000 thoughts, while the same person would see more than 300,000 images per day. Obviously, we are all visually oriented.

61

SEEK STILLNESS, SILENCE AND SUSTAIN

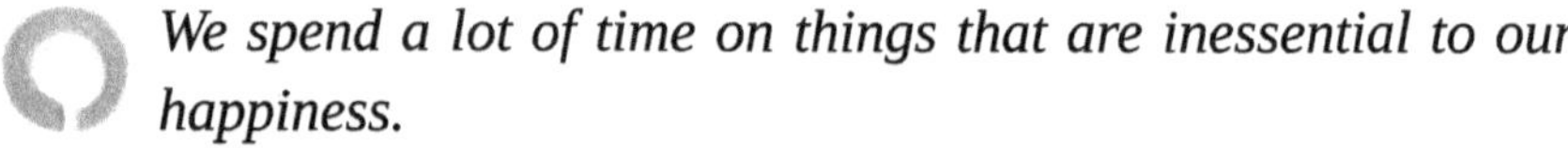 *We spend a lot of time on things that are inessential to our happiness.*

It's more about feeling alive in your everyday life.

At what moments in your life do you feel truly happy or fulfilled?

Sit in **stillness, silence** and think about it for a couple of minutes.

Self-Silencing versus Stillness.

Stillness is a healthy habit of self-awareness; a powerful tool.

The power of **silence** and **stillness** cannot be underestimated.

In fact, it is one of the most powerful forces in the world.

It is the ability to be calm, relaxed and to make an appropriate decision in a complex situation; finding your purpose to get your life in order—even amidst chaos, clamor and commotion.

Once you reach your stillness, you will know what you really need and how to be a better thinker and doer to realize your portent potential.

62

THE INCREDIBLE BENEFITS OF JOURNALING

Keeping a journal is one of the most effective ways to reflect on your daily experiences and make stronger and better decisions.

Writing in a journal allows you to access those innate and innovative ideas hiding within you.

It can strengthen you immensely and ease the symptoms of depression and anxiety.

It stops your mind from going around in circles and can help you make sense of your thoughts, feelings, and emotions.

Write every day:

- What are my feelings right now?
- How do I feel about my work?
- What is the great and profound idea I came across recently? (mine or others')
- What do I love about it and what to do with it? And
- What am I noticing? -and such.

The benefits include deepening your creativity and intuition and clarifying your perspective perfectly.

The Beauty and Benefits of your Journal

The following may sound utterly positive and first-class to believe, but it is a fact of reality.

Crystallizes and clarifies your ideas and insights

Affirms that you can make your ideas and goals real and that your ideas and idealizations will become a reality.

Creative insights, peak state on a regular basis, leading to calculated and systematic productivity.

Specifically, in your daily freewheeling writing session, let your thoughts have the freedom to write about what emerges afresh in your mind of varied kinds. Don't control and refrain from making it sound or seem smart.

You may write about:

How did your previous day go (the good, the bad, etc.)?

What you did well (your 'wins')

What didn't go well (what you didn't do, who you didn't reach out to, where you fell short?)

Record any significant events like great moments with a friend, family, or a breakthrough in your work.

How do you intend to take what you learned from your previous week or days and do better?

Write down your bigger picture goals in a short bullet-point list as a reminder of your goals.

Write your proximal goals (things you're immediately working toward over the next couple of months or sooner).

Write specific to-dos you must do the following week, including plans regarding your morning routine, learning, relationships, work, fitness, etc.

This would help you reconnect deeply with yourself and your definitive purpose, goal, and direction.

To put yourself into a peak state, so that you can achieve the dreams and vision you're seeking in your life.

To frame yourself for what you really want to do, review your life vision and put your day into perspective.

To live proactively, not reactively, so that you avoid self-sabotage.

Doesn't this sound remarkable? Have total faith in yourself to pursue and celebrate the journey of writing a daily journal.

If you read your long-term goals every day, you will think about them every day. If you think about them every day and spend your days working toward them, they'll manifest. A fundamental aspect of that is writing in your journal and reviewing them every single day.

You use your journal for:

Crystallizing and clarifying your ideas and insights

Affirming to yourself that you can make your ideas and goals real affirms that your ideas and idealizations will become a reality.

Make strategic plans to bring your ideas and goals to fruition. Gratefully acknowledging the external factors at play.

Creative insights, peak state on a regular basis, leading to calculated and systematic productivity

Specifically, in your weekly planning session—which should happen *in your journal*—you can write about the following things:

How your previous CV worked (the good, the bad, etc.)

What you did well (your 'wins')

What didn't go well (what you didn't do, who you didn't reach out to, where you fell short?)

Record any significant events (such as great moments with a friend, family, or a breakthrough in your work).

How do you intend to take what you learned from your previous week and do better next week, month or...

Write down your bigger picture goals (in a short bullet-point list as a reminder of your 'why' and 'end' goals).

Write your proximal goals (things you're immediately working toward over the next 1–6 months)

Write specific to-dos you must do the following week (including plans regarding your morning routine, learning, relationships, work, fitness, etc.)

To reconnect deeply with yourself and your why.

To put yourself into a peak state, such that you can achieve the dreams and vision you're seeking in your life.

To frame yourself for what you really want to do

To live proactively, not reactively, so that you avoid self-sabotage.

63

BE SMART. DON'T MISS WHAT YOU DON'T HAVE

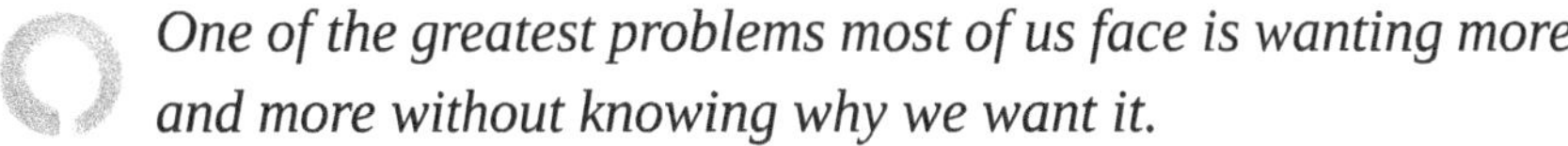 *One of the greatest problems most of us face is wanting more and more without knowing why we want it.*

This leads to unhappiness.

Knowing what and how much is enough is all about finding satisfaction and happiness in what you have.

When you step back and examine what you hope for as against what you have, you will realize that it is entirely useless, inessential or superfluous to want more and more of anything.

<u>64</u>

YOUR CHARISMA CAPTURES OTHERS' ATTENTION

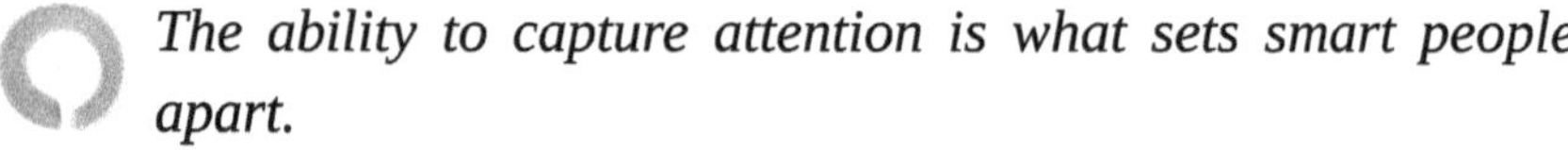 *The ability to capture attention is what sets smart people apart.*

It's all about how you make people feel.

BE PRESENT: To draw people's attention, you have to pay attention to yourself.

When you become more engaged, your audience will become more engaged.

Charisma is when you find and exude positive energy and optimism.

Be a person whose positive energy and optimism lift the moods of those around you.

That's charisma.

Being charismatic is about being able to connect with people and make them feel special.

That starts with being present with yourself, understanding how you're feeling and getting into your rhythm, by being your natural self.

Allow your feelings to flow with what you're saying.

65

WHY WOULD YOU FIGHT WITH YOURSELF?

 *Don't fight with yourself.*

How can you win?

There's no victory or defeat.

It's like creating a conflict between your hands.

"You are within both, and both are within you."

Withdraw from such a situation and become a witness.

When a desire, goal, or interest in a thing is involved, don't get identified with it.

You are much bigger or, in other words, not so small to be identified with those trivial, fleeting, and passing things.

Go through the trivialities in detail, but as a witness, be willing to withdraw from anything that's not suitable or compatible.

Don't lose awareness of your true, beautiful, and smart self.

Prevent depression, dismay, and any of those 'anti' attitudes.

66

EMPTY YOUR MIND
EVERY NOW AND THEN

Regular breaks will not break you.

Make it a practice to have your downtime for an exchange, a connection.

It's about unplugging from the task at hand and being present with your colleagues, friends, or family.

It can be a way to pause, relax, and connect with yourself, your loved ones, music, or a book.

Sprezzatura is an important aspect of your life compared to a night out, watching endless TV shows, gaming or bouts of alcoholic parties and, so on.

Simply immerse yourself in what and who is before you. Doing so can be surprisingly powerful without worrying about other things that are just there, which don't demand your attention right now.

Amazing power is available to us with a clear mind.

67

THERE'S NO SUCH THING AS BAD TIMES

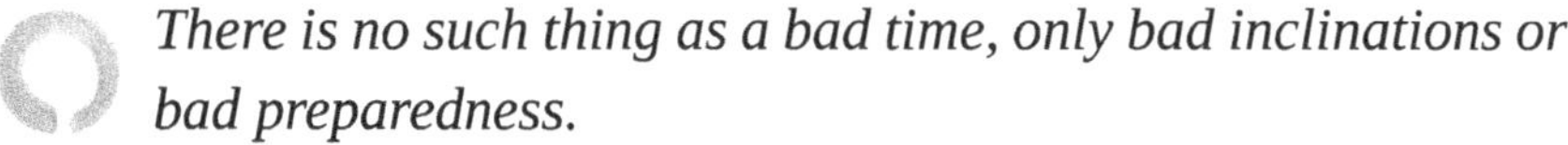 *There is no such thing as a bad time, only bad inclinations or bad preparedness.*

Embrace the weather, stock market, or political situation, not as a terrible thing at any given time.

Focus on getting 'well-adjusted' rather than having any extreme emotions or feelings, because there's no such thing as 'bad'

De-dramatize fears and ever-changing emotional impulses.

Stop giving undue importance to any emotion at a given time and stop wasting your precious time and energy trying to justify or validate it.

Take a balanced and rational approach to do things correctly or, in fact, appropriately.

If need be, take those close to you into confidence and talk about the so-called 'difficult things'.

68

BE MINDFUL

Take pleasure, do your best to enjoy what is right before you right now: work, food, people or whatever else.

When you do this, no matter the circumstances or situation, you will bring out your true self, discover inner peace, and bliss.

Thinking of your work mindfully, you will then think, nurture, and educate yourself in the process.

69

'SHOW OFF' WOULD SWITCH YOU OFF!

Don't ever show off. At the most, it would put others off.

It's wrong and in vain to prove or attempt something for others.

Those are lies and a habitual bad habit you have gotten used to over the years.

Live for and by your true self's intentions, natural flow, and values.

<u>70</u>
THE IMPORTANCE OF WHAT IS IMPORTANT

What's really important? -is an important question to ask yourself whenever you are angry, upset, or uncomfortable with a person, a situation or whatever.

Be flexible, embrace the changes and carry on in your stride.

Your original expectations aren't holy or sacrosanct or of any great importance in the first place.

71

BE DECISIVE TRUSTING YOURSELF

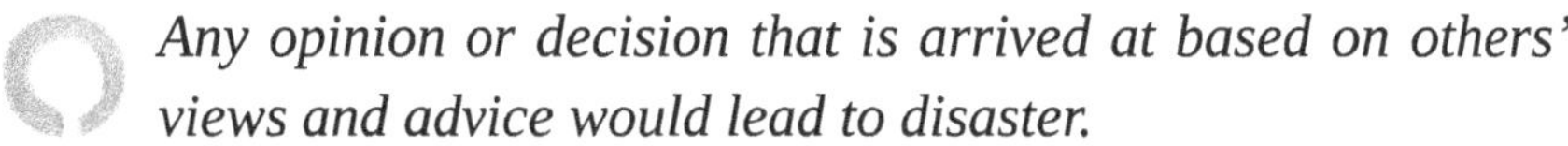 *Any opinion or decision that is arrived at based on others' views and advice would lead to disaster.*

Even husbands and wives make this mistake unknowingly out of sheer habit, as do business associates.

Trust yourself to make decisions with your own realization, knowledge, and experiences.

Neither do you need to nor benefit from conforming to others' diktats, theories, and philosophies.

72
DISCIPLINE IS NOT PUNISHMENT

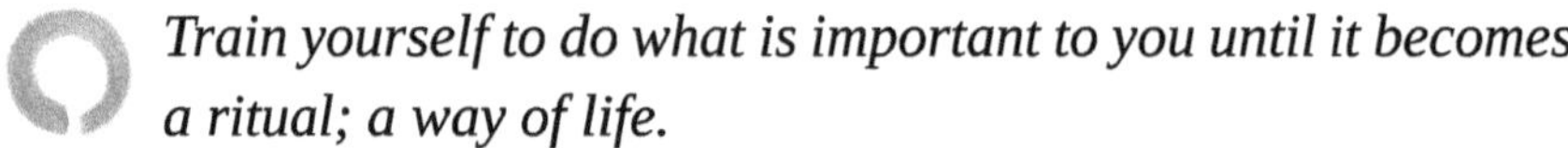 *Train yourself to do what is important to you until it becomes a ritual; a way of life.*

Every successful, rich, and accomplished person through the ages has built a personal ritual.

What's yours?

Work on your habits to make a ritual, and your habits work for you.

73

VALUE YOURSELF MORE

How?

Save your time and yourself, which, in fact, you have been wasting without your knowledge or consent.

Your time is both limited and precious.

When you say 'yes' to someone or something and offer your time, please bear in mind that you are instantly saying 'No' to something that is of great importance to you.

People are wary enough not to part with their cars, money, or other possessions, but they unwittingly and willingly give away their time.

Time, in fact, is more precious and important than money.

When you value your time, you'll end up valuing yourself.

It's not at all rude to say 'no' to save your time and, in turn, yourself.

Save your time and use it wisely.

Please remember and accept the fact that the well-intentioned parents, friends, and others have absolutely no knowledge about you and your innate or potential to do, to 'Have' and 'Be,' in so many aspects, factors, and the worlds so to say.

Yet, it's common human nature to offer unsolicited advice, opinions and suggestions and, so on.

You have to discover with total self-belief fearlessly and with utmost confidence.

You will be shocked to find your revelations.

Believe it, believe in yourself.

74

CHANGE THE WAY YOU
SPEAK TO YOURSELF

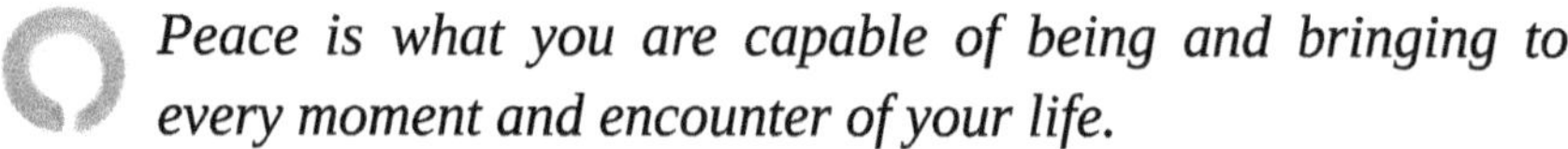 *Peace is what you are capable of being and bringing to every moment and encounter of your life.*

When you have learned to silence your incessant inner dialogue, you attain peace.

Being peaceful isn't dependent on your surroundings nor has anything to do with other people.

Don't look for peace. Instead, stay peaceful.

Peace, harmony, and bliss can't be sought outside.

You have to choose to be.

If you mind your mind, you will never mind the emotions and dramas of your mind, as caused by your encounters with other people.

Self-dialogue is critical and could be harmful.

Did you know the person to whom you would ever talk the most in your lifetime is yourself?

So, speak to yourself as you would to a smart, successful, and savvy person.

If you don't feel you deserve to be spoken to in the best manner, who and how would others?

Change your thoughts, your confidence, and the way you feel about your work and, of course, yourself.

In other words, CURTAIL YOUR INNER DIALOGUE

<u>75</u>

THINKING IS NOT THE SAME AS "WORRYING" AND ACCEPTING YOURSELF IS NOT "GIVING UP"

 *Don't mix your thinking with doubt.*

When you do that, it becomes a worry; a big worry.

Accepting yourself is not giving up.

Prepare yourself to accept reality for what it is.

Seeing things as they are, accepting things as they have become a rarity.

It is entirely within your power to decide how to deal with what happens.

Look at things as they are and not as you would like them to be; meeting your misinformed perceptions and expectations.

People choose to see the way that suits their mind, mood, and manner.

Most people, when they say they are 'thinking', are, in fact, worrying!

When your thinking is mixed with doubts, you are worrying because you have successfully managed to convert normal thoughts into worries.

Have you noticed that we are conditioned to be skeptical, negative, and doubtful about everything and anybody at the outset?

In fact, if it continues for much longer, would harm you, your perceptions, and your life.

<u>76</u>

SEE WHAT IS THERE RATHER THAN WHAT YOU ARE LOOKING FOR

Removing every non-essential element will allow you to be happy, healthy, and productive.

Think and act for yourself.

Choose people, activities, and environments to be your best self.

One thing that is vitally important in your life, over which you have total control, is your thoughts.

Think appropriate to your true self.

Be your natural, divine self and think in tandem to celebrate life.

If you can't do this in and by your mind naturally and willfully, you may be sure you will have absolutely nothing in your capacity to modify.

Discovering yourself is conquering life to your total benefit.

77

NATURE IS A NATURAL POWERHOUSE

 *Nature is a natural powerhouse; the healing power of nature is immense and immortal.*

Bathe yourself in nature: silence, senses, slowing down, sharing, and safety are the considerations.

Be with nature and stay in the present incessantly.

At least, remind yourself to reset to stay in the present according to your natural accord.

You are meant to live in accordance with nature, to avoid any trouble.

Being with nature helps restore inner balance.

Nature bathing is a healing power of nature. There are five basic considerations during nature bathing: Silence, Senses, Slowing down, Sharing and Safety. You would have noticed the five considerations are all indirect outcomes of coming to and staying in the present. The cause of physiological pain and mental anxiety cannot always be found in the body or even in one's immediate environment but can be understood by studying your unconscious or subconscious. Since the body is also made up of elements that can be found in nature, being with nature helps restore inner balance.

If you want to create an art of grass or trees, not only would you have to observe, analyze, study, and be with grass or trees, but you must become grass or trees!

78
LET GO OF... AND LET'S GO

 *What can you let go of?*

We all carry wounds and grudges.

People have wronged us.

We have been hurt.

We have been deprived and so on.

The question is: How long are we going to carry this around?

Every day, we should take a few minutes to think about the baggage we carry around and decide whether to keep carrying it on.

There is plenty we can let go of.

We can forgive.

We can forget.

We can move on.

Be willing and ready to let go.

Don't be adamant about clinging on to anything. Go off-script and believe in yourself, in your innate and incredible abilities of 'versatile flexibility.'

Because no amount of empirical research would support the ground realities as faced by you as you go by. Please be assured that the expression: "let go" does not imply you are weak, incapable or aimless. Conversely, one has to be bold and brave enough to stop an unproductive activity and move on to the smarter, mightier and more appropriate ones.

79

DON'T EVER WASTE YOUR TIME TRYING TO PROVE YOU ARE RIGHT

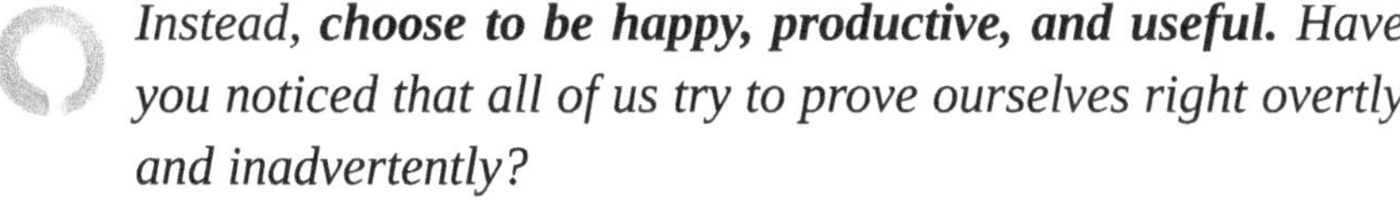 *Instead, **choose to be happy, productive, and useful.** Have you noticed that all of us try to prove ourselves right overtly and inadvertently?*

This is done out of sheer habit; almost on autopilot.

At times, we get carried away seeking the comfort of something or someone, right, imagining such a thing exists. This is an abysmal action to seek comfort, safety, or support; what a mindless thing to do.

Bear in mind that there's no such thing as being right or someone being right (better or great) forever.

Smarter, successful, and millionaire-mindset people would rather choose to be happier first, on their own accord, than prove themselves to be right.

Your happiness is no other people's business, and likewise, we don't need others' endorsement to think, accept, or even be righteous. These are your own individualistic choices and ways of doing things—congruent with your goals, interests, and being.

Embrace the things as they happen in your life, without being judgmental.

Good and bad are relative and subjective based on several factors. After all, there isn't one thing that's absolutely right or totally wrong. What is the point in searching for such a state that doesn't exist and wasting your efforts in dwelling in that virtuous comfort and, added to that, proving 'that' which cannot be proven for it has no substance of worthiness to fight for? It is a colossal waste of your precious time and energy.

Try accepting others as right for a while, and you'll notice the phenomenal changes in your everyday life. You will be loved more by more people, and they will want to do things for you on their own. This may sound incredible in the beginning but is nature's way.

To make this point simpler and clear, think about the things and people who were right, great, and wow when you were younger. They have not changed now nor have they become worse nor are those things rotten now. But you just don't find it right to call them right. Read it again and think about it. So, avoid getting into the futile mindset, experiment, and exercise of searching and labeling anything as right.

<u>80</u>

YOU'D BETTER MAKE YOURSELF BETTER?

Don't waste your time and money on so many things and ways that are on offer to make you feel better. This is a dangerous, hidden, and hideous ploy that could ruin you.

Aren't you ashamed to allow other people, products or even places to be in charge of and responsible for you to feel good? And in addition, paying a premium for it, whatever the promise or premise. Feeling good is your personal and private play. When it is left to be determined by extraneous factors: products, people, and premises, that kind of 'feeling good' with goods cannot last for long nor be satisfactory. It is possible for all of us to be masters of our happiness and all its synonyms. Products, people, and premises are just about a variety of media, menu, and options with promises of portent potential good. Shouldn't we rather choose to be our own masters to decide on the repertoire of all those factors? Happiness, satisfaction, bliss, joy, and so on are left to our own discretion, based on varying factors of our own accord. It is time to respect ourselves.

You can control your mind to master your circumstances and shape the world.

Whatever you consider right now as the source of joy and happiness is just a promise, an excuse, and a projection.

The problem is not seeing happiness as something that you could achieve in your life --all by yourself. Stop seeking outside all the time; just because we have been conditioned to do so.

Make yourself that promise, excuse, and projection that you are happy. Because the source and cause are your perceptions and mood –entirely left up to you.

To understand others and accept new technology, nature, and even happiness, you have got to understand your 'self', or yourself first.

People in general attribute great success and achievements to that unknown something.

That something is understanding yourself.

When that happens, you get to naturally accomplish what you were meant to as a leader, artist, musician, writer, or a statesman.

Check to see every now and then if you think and act as per your original self's intent, thoughts, or true potential.

I doubt it if you are doing so.

You'll be shocked and surprised to know that it is easier to build a beautiful world around you instead of searching for a beautiful world or an idea.

Build your perfect day and your perfect 'self,' every day.

81

LEARN – KEEP LEARNING

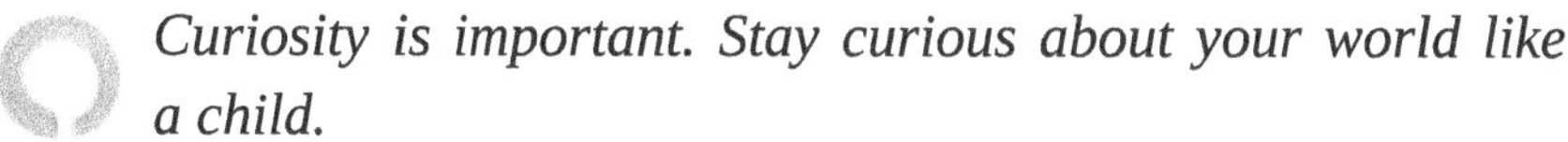 *Curiosity is important. Stay curious about your world like a child.*

Learn anything new and even difficult; the difficulty is something that you have gotten used to accepting habitually. Reverse it and you'll be amazed at the results of indulging in learning and experiencing new stuff.

What the whole exercise does to your total self is wordless and world-class.

It's a combination of fun, joy, knowledge, satisfaction, and revelation; a distinct and direct connection to your true and real self.

Challenge your mind. Make conscious efforts to keep redefining your past habits and history; they being past, over and history, stop holding on to them.

Learn new things: *Take singing and dancing lessons, knowing well not to compete or be compared with the Travoltas and Kumars.*

82

DIFFICULTIES AND DISCOMFORTS ARE ESSENTIAL AND POWERFUL

Maximum development and growth occur at the border of your comfort and discomfort zones.

Push yourself to discomfort frequently to get the best results.

The best thing you could do is to do your best at a given time.

We should do the things we love genuinely and not the things we think we should to impress the outside world.

Stay out of your comfort zone as often as possible.

Learn something totally new. Master it of your own accord. Challenge yourself with the next level of difficulty and discomfort.

Stimulate your brain energy for a sharper mind in you.

Routines and any specific number of habits would make your brain dull and dead.

Difficulty and discomfort include spending time with different people—not necessarily difficult people but from different backgrounds.

Intentionally seek out others who have different interests, careers, or skill sets from diverse social or cultural backgrounds.

Make it a ritual of sorts, suiting your lifestyle; making it a part of your life.

Constantly learn new and crazy things.

It's better to get crazy over new experiences than to go dull, defunct, and crazy, anyway.

Try using a non-dominant hand for day-to-day work. Write with your other hand; challenging, fun, and highly useful to connect with yourself and to stay in the present. Engage your mind, body, and soul to stay alive and fresh.

<u>83</u>

RESTFULNESS IS NOT LAZINESS

 *Don't allow yourself to be confused.*

Resting and restfulness are highly important and very useful.

The whole world is madly active, trying to reach somewhere; not really being aware of where or what's important.

Learn to relax and rest truly to gain more insight into yourself.

You will become calmer, more confident, and more productive as well.

Great wisdom, relaxed spontaneity, quiet optimism, and gentle humor are the natural outcome when you are rested and relaxed.

It will change your work; it will be more artistic and more useful.

You will shy away from unnecessary trivia.

You will also say only what is needed to be said.

So, what is the best way to rest or relax?

The only name for that rightful way is MEDITATION.

84

LEARN TO LISTEN INTENTLY

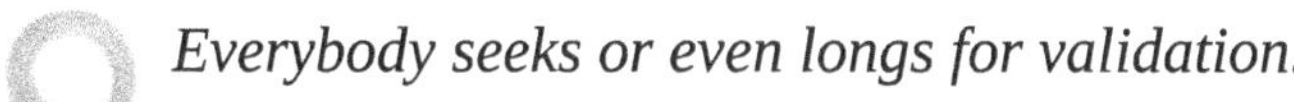 *Everybody seeks or even longs for validation.*

So, you'd better learn to listen and listen intently–whether you like it or not.

Because it is worth it.

This is yet another secret that's simple: To succeed, remember the common fact that every person you go to, interact with, and work with longs for validation. Validation of their views, voices to be heard, opinions appreciated, and them being respected.

This applies to people from all walks of life in our sphere.

This may sound so silly and simple, yet it is an important and incredible insight to remember to just simply get by or move on successfully in your endeavors. You may choose to decide.

(An interesting point to explore and refer to is the fact that an average person speaks at 225 words per minute, but one can listen to up to 500 words per minute)

85

HABITS, ROUTINES AND BEHAVIORS ARE NOT ONE AND THE SAME NOR REPLACEABLE

There has always been confusion over this.

One of the prime reasons and fundamental causes of ill health is a horrifying truth, hard to accept: wrong habits.

'Habits' are not in the common way the habits have been understood.

It is the 'wrong habit of thoughts', giving expression and multiple dimensions to negatives that cause and complement ill health.

Can you believe it?

Sometimes the best way to rest is to do something that tires you out, as many voluntary hobbies illustrate.

- High-Intensity Training
- Swimming
- Martial Arts and
- more vide your interests

About 45 minutes of physical exercise, intentional learning of any chosen field of activity when done regularly, you will be amazed at the outcome.

In fact, it is a perfect activity synchronizing the mind, body and spirit. Such exercises are wholesome, providing a holistic experience.

<u>86</u>

BEWARE OF YOUR ENVIRONMENT

 *Do you choose the environments you live in?*

Seldom, or is it possible to have a choice?

Like the word 'habit', environment too is a major reason and influencer of your overall well-being, including your fame and fortune.

Unfavorable environment influences all of us from our childhood.

The important fact or aspect to remember is the role played by the kinds and quality of people in your environment.

This may sound dastardly or disturbing, but it is a fact that influences the human mind's sensory feelings.

The quality of your life is determined by the quality of people in your environment in every way.

Of course, the environments by themselves do play a very big and important role, which is discussed elsewhere in these pages.

"If you do not create and control your environment, your environment controls you."

Not so surprisingly, the environment contributes to our happiness, contentment, and even productivity. The city of Paris makes us fashionable or at least fashion-conscious, while New York or Tokyo would make us fast-paced; even make us walk faster. Choose the environment that is complementary to your core values, interests, capabilities, and even goals.

Build your environment of physical ambience and the kind/mix of people in it.

In the context of environments, the people you choose to be with matter and, in fact, determine who you are becoming and what you are achieving.

In retailing/shopping, the importance of the environment created by the respective brand cannot be simplified because the environments make the shoppers feel and behave in a particular way, prompting them to buy with confidence, pride, and joy.

Try selling the product elsewhere, for example on the curbs of a crowded street.

The restaurant's ambience or environment makes it successful and right to enjoy the gourmet delights.

The most important and often ignored point in the right environments is the mix of people in it. In fact, in most environments or cases, the people make an important contribution to the value, ambience, and even the price you pay!

So, when you know that your environment determines your growth, goals, success and happiness, isn't it obvious that you have the choice to decide on the people in your environment?

Right now, decide the kind of people you must stop meeting and wasting time. That itself would pave the way to the right people who need to be there in your environment. People play important roles in your places; your environment. Period.

<u>87</u>

GIVE YOURSELF A MEDIA BREAK.
BAN THE MEDIA!

Censor, limit, restrict, and ration what you hear and see in every form of media if you want peace, harmony, and more productivity from yourself.

Overindulgence in others' opinions and projections with typical blockbuster movie-style mastery is rotten, rubbish, and redundant.

Don't voluntarily or unknowingly give in and commit dastardly mistakes. Or are they a part of bad habits?

We are oblivious to the fact that about 96% of what's happening around all of us is positive, encouraging, progressive, and insightful or at least neutral.

Why waste your precious time trying to know various versions of the undesirable 4%?

When you while away your precious time and opportunities in others' dramatic, fictitious projections, you are not giving yourself any chance for the easily available potential for your happiness and success.

Clear your mind of accumulated information that does not serve you.

Our reactions and responses are based on our moods and experiences.

Your thoughts and emotions could help you live your life in your best state.

When you learn to do this and reset your 'self', you will succeed in any facet of your life.

88

MONEY BY ITSELF DOES NOT ASSURE HAPPINESS

Money doesn't assure happiness. What everyone wants is not money but fulfilling dreams. Realizing desires, dreams, or goals is more important than mere money, besides good, loving relationships of mutual trust. Money is not replaced nor made redundant, but the point is the innate need to get our dreams and goals fulfilled, which is of immense and innate need for all of us.

Identify the goodies and rewards that money just can't buy.

Don't habituate more easily and readily to things money can buy than to things money cannot.

Avoid clinging to material things rather than to relationships; meaningful relationships would beat anything that money could buy, hollow.

Little do we realize or accept the fact that when we make more friends, we give ourselves a great gift of possibilities that determine our happiness and success.

<u>89</u>

STOP, SUBTRACT, AVOID
THE NON-ESSENTIALS

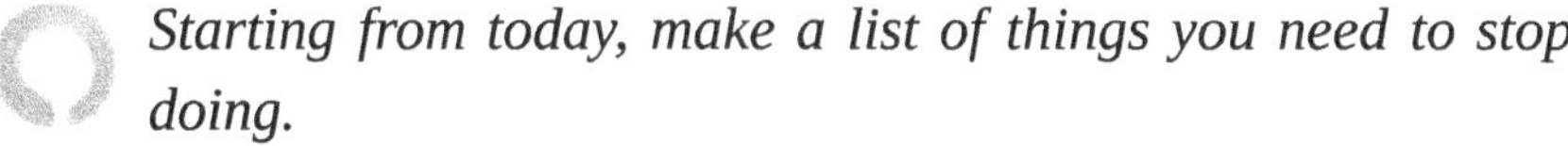 *Starting from today, make a list of things you need to stop doing.*

It's not that you have been smart in making a list of things to do and keeping it up successfully. Get into the habit of stopping at least one thing that you have gotten used to and are currently continuing to do, oblivious to any reason or purpose.

Nothing clears itself; especially rubbish, useless, and the non-essentials.

Plan to STOP doing things, starting in a small way.

SILENCE: Silence and stillness or calmness are among the most powerful forces in the world. They are the ability to be calm, relax, and make appropriate decisions in complex situations, to find your purpose, and to get your life in order—even amidst chaos and pressure. Once you reach and realize stillness, you will know what you need and how to be a better thinker and a better doer.

<u>90</u>

THE WORLD DOESN'T FUNCTION ACCORDING TO YOUR PRESUMPTIONS, ASSUMPTIONS, OR IMAGINATION

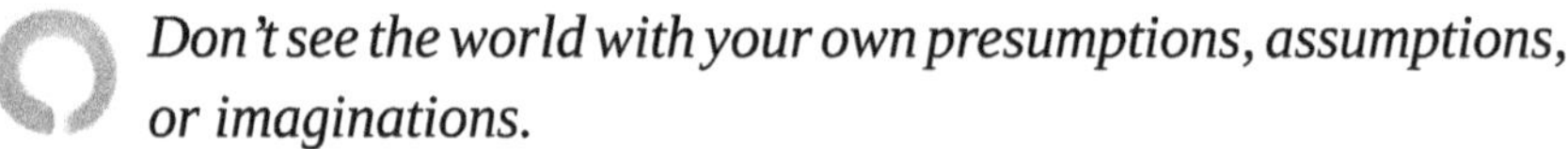 *Don't see the world with your own presumptions, assumptions, or imaginations.*

You need more of those who are insightful, experienced and who have crossed the rivers (done things) to get to see the world in its true reality. Obviously, you will show discretion and be selective.

When you do so, you will end up seeing things so differently, beautifully and profitably, too.

91
CHANGE YOUR HABITS REGULARLY

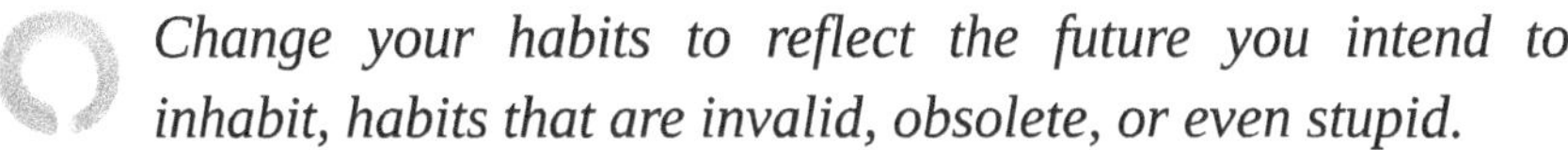 *Change your habits to reflect the future you intend to inhabit, habits that are invalid, obsolete, or even stupid.*

Delete the behaviors, activities, and relationships that reflect your present normal that are no longer interesting or progressive compared to where you plan on going. Pursue those things which completely align with the future you want to have or create.

Say NO to everything else.

Aim to grow and disrupt what is currently a boring norm.

92

ENJOY YOUR BODY AS IT IS

Be aware of your body and its movements.

Train your body to do what's seemingly difficult or impossible.

Train your body to remove the word 'difficult' from your lexicon.

Understand that your body is not what you believe it to be.

Change your belief.

It's far more resilient and versatile.

Think of yourself as strong, accept your body as it is, accept the fact that there's nothing wrong with it and in you.

Keep in mind it would show, reflecting what you constantly think, telling yourself and your beliefs.

93

BREATHE – BREATHE – BREATHE EASY AND NATURALLY

This may sound obvious and silly. When you are caught up in the desired results, you cannot enjoy the beautiful life in the 'here and now' and breathe unnaturally and even with some difficulty.

Don't place a value judgment on what you are doing at the moment with anxiety on the results.

Think about it: Would you judge if your 'breathing pattern' is good or bad?

Do not divide and judge things as they are not bipolar.

Correct breathing techniques are very important to get rid of stress and negative energies.

Your breathing pattern changes according to your mental state.

You tend to breathe heavily if you are angry, upset, or disappointed.

That's because your mental state affects your breathing pattern.

The good news is you have total control and command over your breathing pattern to achieve your natural and peaceful state.

94

THE PAST IS A PAST SENTENCE, THE FUTURE PERFECT

The less tied you are to the past, the bigger your confidence.

The bigger your confidence, the less you identify with who you were and the more you identify with who you intend to be.

The first step in this direction is eliminating the stuff in your life that you clearly know you don't want.

Remove that bunch of stuff, including certain people in your 'environment' that don't match the future you deserve.

That single act will ignite your confidence.

When your confidence is high, deep in your soul, whatever goal you set, you are going to figure out a way to make it happen.

You will be completely committed to results without caring how long it takes because you are happy every moment in the present in your pursuit.

Learn to attain the goal but don't attach any desire to it, wasting your thoughts and mind in the future.

This is a usual flow or habit that you can do away with to boost your well-realized confidence.

Confidence and faith are synonymous. Confidence will lead to success when you act in accordance with your true self's desires.

Faith and confidence without action or work are dead.

Combining your confidence with a definitive purpose in what you're doing means you are committed, have direction, and the will to do what it takes to succeed.

When you pursue what you genuinely desire and value, regardless of the outcomes along the way, you'll enjoy going forward until you succeed.

You cannot be confident if you are not congruent with what you're doing in strict alignment with your true self.

It's easy to get caught up in the thick of thin things.

For you to pursue and succeed at the right things, you need to be connected to your deeper, more intuitive self.

Meditation helps you to stay connected to your 'self'.

It's all about being really connected to yourself, the moment, and the right people.

That's when your success is assured.

It doesn't happen by putting in long hours, working hard, and connecting with all the wrong people.

Be clear on your WHY.

Completing the tasks daily increases your confidence.

When you become congruent and eliminate everything in your life that doesn't match, and when you become a power finisher of everything you believe you should do, then your confidence and your future take off and are assured with certainty.

Nothing can stop you.

We give too much importance to what we have gone through and accomplished in the past. We assume that in the future, we will mostly continue to be who we are now. Look back some years ago and compare it with where you are currently to understand that your past is not prevalent in predicting who you will be and could be in the future.

Stop attaching yourself so much to the person you think you are. Your future self is going to be way beyond and totally different from your routine limited notion based on your past. Change is inevitable. Embrace change. Growth is your option for the taking. Imagine, visualize, and believe in your better future. It is real.

> One of the assured ways to stay and experience the present is by pursuing what you have never done before. Besides setting and going after bigger goals, explore to experience far bigger things, far too different from your routine or wrongly presumed mindset with limited imaginations and capabilities.

You are complete just by yourself. Your real self is waiting to be discovered. Thoughts determine the quality of our lives; they determine our problems and achievements.

Work, success, relationships, happiness, everything depends on the way we think.

Think about it. Have you given enough thought to your thoughts?

> Have you understood the answers in y/our thoughts and how thoughts themselves could be affected or influenced in the appropriate way?

Review your thoughts.

Know how you think and how to improve your thoughts.

Improve the thinking.

Think of your own right way to accelerate life.

Is that possible?

How?

When you change your thoughts, you learn how to change your life.

When you choose to be happy, your negatives shift to positives.

The stories we tell ourselves make up our identity and dictate what we believe we can and cannot do.

Find the cause of your problem and eliminate it.

To change your thinking and life, you cannot stay in your comfort zone.

You need to take risks until you get comfortable with those risks, then take more.

The more you push yourself, the easier it will become to write or rewrite your story and transform your life.

> When you move from your comfort zone to the beginning of discomfort and pain, your focus and attention or even your perspective change totally because of your intense focus on the only 'one' as taken by your mind. When you return to your comfort zone, you will realize your real self.

95

WRITE YOUR CV REGULARLY AND TIME AND, AGAIN

This is not for the purpose of seeking, applying, and securing employment. There are numerous other benefits when you write and revise your CV periodically.

Think about the time you wanted to impress the girl you were in love with. At that point in time, you would have been keen and excited to highlight certain aspects of yourself and your personality as in your CV. The same CV as a communication tool would have been invalid for your first job; possibly a part-time job. Later on, you would have learned to complement your prospects as per their area of business, interest, values and so on.

Now, I am asking you to write your CV periodically and, in fact, far too frequently. You will be amazed to know how it works, sounds, and looks, getting you benefits of immense value and, most importantly, what it does to your mind in setting goals with a definitive purpose. Detail the nuts and bolts on specifically how you could use your CV on a regular basis to achieve any goal, however big, audacious, and lofty.

Focus on the **continuous process** of using your CV to shape and achieve your goals. This may sound preposterous but is so axiomatic.

The updating and revising of your CV portion is where you solidify, clarify, affirm, and strategize your insights, goals, and plans. This will be a major introspection exercise to plan your future more efficiently and effectively.

Momentum leads to confidence, which then leads to bigger and bigger dreams, better service, and value you can provide, and to lead a more congruent life.

Your CV is your most powerful resource for manifesting your dreams. Writing your CV complements and deepens the essential activities of meditation, visualization, and prayer.

If you're serious about achieving specific and big things in your life, you need to put yourself into a peak state and make a firm decision from that state. Usually, that will require getting out of your normal, day-to-day routine, where you can gain clarity. Every morning, you can use your CV to prime yourself into the person you need to be—that day, and every day—in order to make your dreams a reality.

You do this by writing your goals and dreams down in the affirmative every time. You then write down all the ideas, thoughts, plans, and strategies that come to your mind about what you need to do in order to achieve those goals. In your CV, you will write them as though you have already overcome and achieved. You write down the distractions you need to remove from your life that are stopping you from getting where you need to go.

You also use your CV for ideation and creation. Your brain is very creative, and your subconscious mind is very susceptible when it comes to an important thing like a CV. While writing about your ideas, you'll get a ton of creative breakthroughs that will enable you to do amazing work.

96

DON'T EVER GET CAUGHT UP IN THE FUTURE

When you move from your comfort zone, or when you are caught up in the future, wanting to produce profits or results, you are unable to devote yourself to the here and now.

Conversely, choose to get caught up in the here and now, doing whatever needs to be done, without getting caught up in the results and their benefits.

When you do that, your anxieties will vanish regarding reaping the desired benefits, achieving the best results that you deserve.

There is no alternative and you can't go wrong.

When you are **doing**, **thinking**, and **being** in the here and now, be assured that there's no better way than whatever you are up to.

Evaluating or defining things as good or bad and constantly focusing on the benefits is nothing more than being selfish, greedy, and insecure.

97

DO NOT ANTICIPATE TROUBLES OR WORRIES

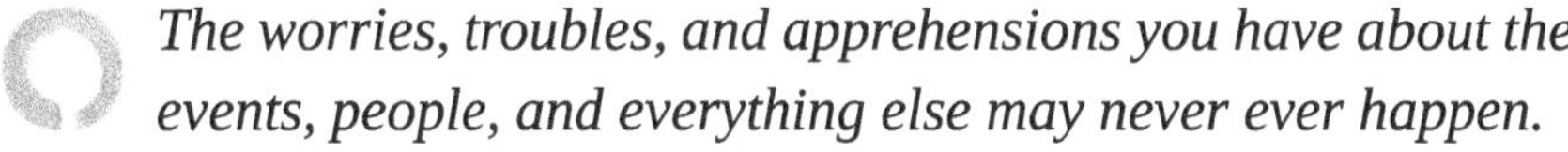 *The worries, troubles, and apprehensions you have about the events, people, and everything else may never ever happen.*

According to studies, about 96% of such events do not ever happen.

Stop wasting your time and energy thinking about it or preparing to deal with it; like finding solutions for non-existent problems.

Please understand that when your thoughts and behavior are preoccupied with imaginary troubles, you may not be ready to receive, realize, and enjoy the abundance in life.

Change your thoughts to love, kindness, peace and joy, and you'll attract more of the same.

Human tendency is to prepare for the worst, as per their projected imaginations and apprehensions. This is a colossal waste of time and effort; absolute rubbish. Secondly, how could anyone be absolutely 'right' in figuring out what is going to be 'wrong'?

98

HAVE YOU GOTTEN IN TOUCH WITH YOURSELF RECENTLY?

Get in tune with yourself and with the changing changing times, and you will get rewarded accordingly. We need a vision to help us focus on our own strengths. If you have that vision, it's much easier to say no to unimportant options and focus on what is important: the essential few. You also need to have a willpower to change your behavior. When you have both, you will complete the job and realize your goals sooner.

Fill your life with interesting experiences. Try important tasks that are supposedly difficult, unclear, and contain emotions of uncertainty. Uncertainty by itself does not mean failure. But even if so, success, too, lies only in the uncertain zones. Any task you undertake for the first time, you'll encounter negative emotions such as fear of failure. Embrace that fact and trust yourself that it's much easier to do this than to do something easier or nothing. It's much better to try and fail than not try at all. Trying but not focusing or attaching to the results can help you decrease the emotions around the risk of failure. What is important and beautifully enriching or joyous is the very act of doing the essential few.

SPREZZATURA leads you to conscious raising, taking control of one's life, heightened self-awareness.

I am not going to make lofty claims but share what I have realized, so that you too could retain it forever to celebrate your life as you were meant to: fulfilled happiness and success.

SPREZZATURA helps you understand yourselves more fully and learn a great deal about who you are and how you react in the world in a short time. It is a source of self-discovery and enlightenment, total concentration, and disciplined daily life.

Attempt new things: new experiences, any source of learning constantly.

Be confident and peaceful. Have faith and fun.

SPREZZATURA would help you stay away from constant delusions and illusions.

"You have power over your mind –not outside events. Realize this, and you will find strength." Source: unknown.

The problem is that our **brains** are good at learning from bad experiences but bad at learning from good experiences.

99

LIVE YOUR LIFE OF SPREZZATURA

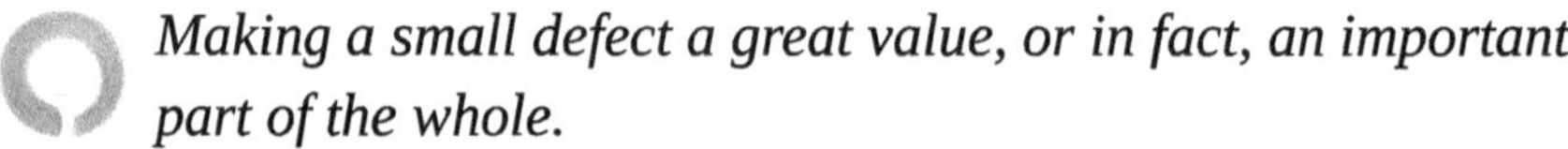 *Making a small defect a great value, or in fact, an important part of the whole.*

Live your life of sprezzatura with a certain nonchalance, so as to conceal all efforts and make whatever you do or say appear to be without effort and yet beautiful, professional or great!

Focusing on high-quality,*haute couture,*fine designs and fine living rather than relying on trendy item

Even in art, sprezzatura way is about creating a sense of ease and effortless beauty, even in complex compositions or technically challenging works.For example, a portrait might feature a subject with a dishevelled look but still exude a sense of grace and charm.

Ultimately, sprezzatura is about finding the balance between effort and outcome, creating a thing or completing a job that is both sophisticated and relaxed.It's a philosophy that emphasizes confidence, ease, and a willingness to **embrace imperfection.**

This can involve:

Quality over quantity

Casual elegance

Deliberate imperfection

Confidence and ease

Cultivate nonchalance

Here's a nonchalance *cheat sheet* to get you started living the Sprezzatura way:

- Displaying a casual and composed demeanor
- Not getting overly flustered or panicky when things don't go as planned
- Surrounding yourself with people and things that make you feel at ease
- Wearing clothes that you feel comfortable and confident in
- Bringing a kind, unruffled, even waggish attitude to the workplace
- Seeking out meditative activities that enhance self-awareness and promote a sense of calm
- The rehearsed spontaneity, studied carelessness, and well-practiced naturalness that underlies persuasive discourse.

(The opposite of sprezzatura is affectation)

<u>100</u>

NOW, IT IS YOUR TURN
OR OPPORTUNITY TO EXPRESS
YOUR SPREZZATURA PRINCIPLE

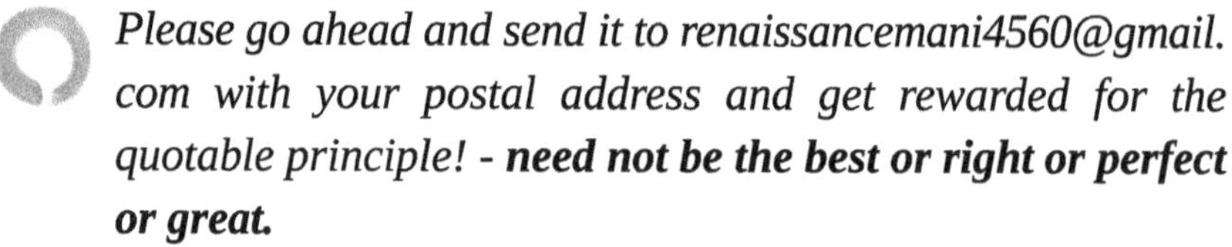 *Please go ahead and send it to renaissancemani4560@gmail. com with your postal address and get rewarded for the quotable principle! - **need not be the best or right or perfect or great.***

Trust yourself.

Thank you.

A Great New Beginning